WHEN EMOTIONS RUN RAMPANT

How Ordinary People Recover from Loss and Get Back to Living

KAREL MURRAY & CAMMIE REED

WHEN EMOTIONS RUN RAMPANT
by Karel Murray & Cammie Reed

Copyright © 2023 Karel Murray and Cammie Reed. All rights reserved. No portion of this book may be reproduced mechanically, electronically, or by any other means, including photocopying, without written permission of the publisher. It is illegal to copy this book, post it to a website, or distribute it by any other means without permission from the authors and publisher.

ISBN: 978-1-948261-66-1
Library of Congress Control Number: 2023912614
Karel Murray (816) 400-7120
E-Mail: Karel@Murray76.com

Cammie Reed (202) 262-0070 E-Mail:

Hope@GrievingHeart.com Website:

www.HopeGrievingHeart.com

Interior & Cover Design by DianeWoodsDEsign.com

Limits of Liability and Disclaimer of Warranty

The authors and publisher shall not be liable for your misuse of this material. This book is strictly for informational and educational purposes.

Warning—Disclaimer

The purpose of this book is to educate and entertain. The authors and/or publisher do not guarantee that anyone following these techniques, suggestions, tips, ideas, or strategies will engender success. The authors and/or publisher shall have neither liability nor responsibility to anyone with respect to any loss or damage caused, or alleged to be caused, directly or indirectly by the information contained in this book.

PRAISE FOR WHEN EMOTIONS RUN RAMPANT

"I read *When Emotions Run Rampant* in just a few hours and felt moved by the many stories of grief, sadness, and despair. Each of us has our own life burdens to carry and the stories and advice here filled me with hope, and a recognition that we all have stories to share if we're brave enough to do so. Thank you for sharing your stories and revealing the vulnerabilities you have. It's so important that each of us realize our own strengths and weaknesses and how we can use those to help ourselves and others."

Debra Hernandez, President, and CEO of DWH Consulting, Inc.

"*When Emotions Run Rampant* is an insightful book that encourages one to "walk through the fire" of grief, so one can move forward with life and take comfort in the memories of the past while embracing the future with positive feelings of self-worth. The stories in the book are honest and transparent. Josh's story and Fred's story were particularly moving. Karel's story about the grief that comes from growing old highlighted that even small events in our lives bring on strong emotions, and our emotions are real. We may not be able to control the event or the emotions, but we do have control over how we respond. The ending sums it up perfectly, "You are worthy.""

Kim Stotesbury, Director KimCo Real Estate Services

"*When Emotions Run Rampant* is a book that took me on quite a journey. Spending quality time with this book allowed me to ask myself questions I had been putting off about my life. Through amazing stories from others, I was able to relate to the roller coaster of emotions shared and find a several solutions that are working for me."

Laurie Guest, CSP, Customer Service Expert, Keynote Speaker, Author

"It is impossible to imagine anyone who has not dealt with the issues and emotions that Karel and Cammie so honestly and openly discuss in *When Emotions Run Rampant*. The numerous personal stories shared throughout this work are palpable, touching, and inspirational. Beyond the honesty and vulnerabilities that each of us carry, this book helps to provide insight and practical solutions to those situations. Learning to shift perspectives, logically identify the core problems, rebound from turmoil, and implement plans of action are all priceless information. I hope that readers find this book in their times of greatest need, and I pray that those readers pass its practical solutions and activities on to their friends and loved ones who may be in turmoil. I cannot thank the authors enough for not only confronting the darkness, but figuring out how each of us can illuminate a path forward."

Leonard C. Elder, JD, DREI, Director of Education & Licensing, North Carolina Real Estate Commission

"A small book but powerful tool that walks you through the grieving process. The information forces you to revisit the painful moments in your life and how it affects who you are today. The book makes you understand that healing is a process and that it starts with knowledge. This is a life changing book. A great read."

Lanice Hall, Missionary, Mount Olive AME Church

"This book is a MUST read. It is well written and easy to understand and relate to the personal stories. Grief is all too common in the world we live in. The authors helped me understand the stages of grief but more importantly how to address my grief in healthy ways. I truly enjoyed the anecdotal stories and appreciate the authors vulnerability of telling their own personal stories. In a post COVID world and so much negative media, everyone should learn how to cope with grief and reading *When Emotions Run Rampant* is a great place to start."

LaKisa Carter, Veteran of the U.S. Air Force and Managing Broker in Maryland

"*When Emotions Run Rampant* is a relevant and timely book that reflects a shared pain left by grief experiences and felt by so many. It not only reminds us that we are not alone, but that Hope is on the healing journey with us!"

Dean Margaree Coleman-Carter, Montclair State University and AME Church Member

Dedication

Thirty-five years ago, a Senior Vice President of the insurance company I worked for stepped into my office and closed the door. He put a photo of a five-year-old child on my desk. As he laid his finger on the image, he looked me in eye and declared, "This is the last time I was truly happy as a child. My alcoholic parents tarnished my outlook on life and trampled my self-esteem until I learned about grief and recovered my self-esteem. You carry a weight that is visible in your drive to be exceptional at all things. I want you to know I see you; I appreciate you. You've nothing to prove to others. Be yourself and enjoy the ride."

That moment changed the course of my life—an act of kindness and release. This book is dedicated to him.

Karel Murray

It was 1996, my life would take a pivotal turn and I would never be the same. I became a griever exposed to the pain of losing my mother, and I had to learn how to live without her. This was the beginning of my journey of healing from loss and learning that life goes on.

I dedicate this book to my mom.

Cammie Reed

CONTENTS

Introduction 11

Chapter 1
The Strongest of Emotions—Grief Defined 17

Chapter 2
Stages of Processing Strong Emotions 23

Chapter 3
Signs of Being Emotionally Overwhelmed 81

Chapter 4
Addressing and Rebounding from Emotional Turmoil 91

Chapter 5
Embracing Inconvenience – Living a Quality Life 105

Chapter 6
Quest for Healing 119

Chapter 7
Transitioning and Releasing the Real You 123

"One who journeys into a strange land, can never return unchanged."

—*C. S. Lewis*

INTRODUCTION

The world we live in and the lives we lead seem to be filled with many uncertainties. We may be happily enjoying our day, when suddenly, something happens that completely changes our plans or expectations. From past experiences, we have learned how to cope with chaos, and we hope our process can work for you to bring comfort and ease back into your life.

Why this book and why now.

In January 2023, both Cammie and Karel attended an educational summit in Scottsdale even though neither of them wanted to truly be there. However, with the encouragement of loved ones, they showed up. On the second day, Karel observed Cammie, sitting alone eating her breakfast. Karel approached asking if she could sit with Cammie. During their conversation, Cammie revealed her sister, Sandra, had been hospitalized for almost two weeks and a nephew had died earlier in the month. She had just attended his funeral.

To add to her heavy emotional load, Cammie had received disappointing news about a video review which was for a speaking certification. In this video, she had shown raw emotions, telling her story of losing her mother. To have the video rejected with no constructive feedback seemed unbearable, especially when Cammie expressed vulnerability.

The catalyst for writing this book came as a result of the conversation between Karel and Cammie.

We know we aren't alone in trying to deal with grief, lost purpose, or other life setbacks.

Karel's Story

As we get older, we realize that we have begun to live our lives defensively, working continually to overcome obstacles wherever and however they appear. What is most disturbing is that the degree of the "explosion" or level of disruption due to an incident or circumstance can't be anticipated, and the resulting emotional or physical carnage can significantly alter our outlook on life in general.

For example, recently my senior-citizen husband stumbled and fell on his hip in the bleachers while several people looked on. His look of chagrin said it all as he quickly hopped up and dusted his jeans off. For an instant, we both understood that as we age, this type of thing will happen more often, and we recognize we are becoming one of "those people"—the old person you must watch out for. The incident was quick, less than thirty seconds, but the emotional impact of embarrassment and realization of our frailty and diminishment of physical vigor could create an opportunity for negative thinking, lowered self-esteem and yes, grief for the youth we have lost.

While this may seem like a minor incident, haven't you noticed that society seems to be latching onto "emotional triggers" and magnifying situations, conversations, or interactions into unfathomable catastrophic events? The COVID pandemic did considerable harm to our population through isolation, which in turn induced fear, paranoia, reckless abandon for society norms and sadness for the loss of intimacy and connection we used to enjoy without any hesitation. What are we supposed to do with that? What happened to personal resilience, perseverance, ducking our head down and plowing forward regardless of the adversity we face?

CAMMIE'S STORY

When my mom died, I felt so lonely even when I was in a room filled with people. I did not know what it was like to lose someone. My oldest sister died when I was sixteen years old and because she was much older and had moved away to start her own family, I imagined that she was in a far-away country. I allowed my mind to take me into another reality where I did not have to deal with her loss. It was denial, and with it, I did not have to accept the death of my sister.

My mom, however, lost her oldest child, and she had to find the strength to go on with life. I remember right next to my mom's chair was a picture of my sister. Next to it was a small vase with one stem of a fresh flower. The fresh flower was a way of keeping my sister's memory alive. Reflecting on my childhood, I am glad that my mother showed me how to grieve by remembering the person.

After my mom's death, I wanted to learn everything I could about the feelings of grief and bereavement. These were words that I have never used before, and I was almost dumbfounded that I didn't know the meaning of these words. The feelings were surfacing faster than I could make sense of what was happening. There were moments where I could not feel anything. It was almost three months after my mother's death before I shed my first tear. The grief was there. I just did not know that I was in a state of shock and numbness. I wanted to cry, but I could not. Somehow, I thought if I cried then I would grieve. What was not happening outwardly was happening inwardly. I was in emotional pain. I was numb, lonely, frustrated, angry, anxious, sad, depressed, and all these feelings were coming at the same time. I thought I was crazy. Emotional pain can be worse than physical pain.

What helped was writing about my feelings, which I still have in my journals. I was able to express my thoughts and feelings in a safe space. I engaged in talk therapy on a weekly basis and attended support groups for about two years. Reaching out for help was extremely therapeutic in my healing process.

Grieving what was or who we were drains us emotionally. We are saddened because of people we have lost, relationships that have stalled or fractured, unfulfilling work or demeaning treatment from those we love and respect. Each of these emotions take a toll on us. It changes us, and impacts everything and everyone we come in touch with. The first step is recognizing the feelings, and once this happens, then we can do something about what is causing us to become emotionally charged.

It's time for us to speak up and have the dialog we need to have to not only learn how to handle the multiple aspects of grief, but to help rebuild our community as it shifts into today's realities. We have learned how to cope effectively with life circumstances in a way that incorporates personal accountability and maintains strong self-esteem, which in turn enables us to recognize the power of our own sense of self-worth and value. It's time for all of us to understand what makes us "tick" as an individual, determine what we have control over and learn to get past our pride in asking for help when we need it.

Our goal in this book is to share our stories and stories of others who have gone through losses that could have been a setback in life. Instead, through perseverance and determination, we have developed skills for survival.

There are times when people are not aware of the symptoms of grief because grieving is a natural process. When a loved one dies, the feelings are overwhelming. The person goes into a state of numbness as a way of surviving and coping through the loss. The numbness helps the person get through the immediate steps of planning the service and making the final preparations. But it's not only the loss of a loved one that creates numbness; it can also come from loss of a relationship, illness, job, divorce, lack of financial stability and so many other areas in a person's life.

Handling grief begins with understanding what grief is and how it can invade all aspects of our lives if we are not aware of the symptoms. Recognizing the signs of grief and then developing skills to overcome the side effects of prolonged grief is our purposeful intention in authoring this book. We will share personal stories as well as references to provide relevance and meaning for you.

After reading this book, it's our hope that you will have a framework to take a realistic inventory of your emotions as they change ever so frequently and can damage personal relationships. By doing the hard work, going through the process, embracing spirituality, and strengthening personal connections to others, we hope you will be able to say, "My feelings are real, I will get through this." It's a natural process to feel pain and hurt after losing someone or experiencing a traumatic loss. One day, however, you will be able to declare, "I am better."

Chapter 1
The Strongest of Emotions- Grief Defined

The best way to start this conversation of rampaging emotions and developing the ability to work through them, in the many stages, is to define the word grief. It is the strongest of emotions.

According to the Mayo Clinic: "Grief is ... an overwhelming emotion for people, regardless of whether their sadness stems from the loss of a loved one or from a terminal diagnosis they or someone they love to have received. They might find themselves feeling numb and removed from daily life, unable to carry on with regular duties while saddled with their sense of loss" (2016).

This definition's focus is on the words "overwhelming emotion." The image we get is of a person huddled in a corner with their head burrowed in their arms, finding it extremely difficult to engage with others or enjoy their life. They have plunged down a massive hole with slick sides and can see no way to climb out. For some, this type of feeling can last for years. When a person is not living the quality of life, it's time to seek help. Help can come in many forms: talking to a friend, journaling your feelings, seeking counseling from your church or another professional. Asking for help is not a form of weakness; rather it is coming from a position of strength.

What about the negative underlying emotions that chisel every day at our well-being that are a result of ongoing abusive situations like abandonment, criticism, bullying, physical impairment because of a disease or accident? We need to acknowledge that we do feel sadness if we can't reach our full potential due to lack of financing, familial support, community opportunities, or discrimination. All may be areas we can't control, but we know they are real in putting roadblocks in our way to achieving our dreams.

Grief is easily understood for the catastrophic events in our lives, but we must acknowledge that an ongoing factor impacting us can also be a result of the accumulation of all the small slights, missteps, life shifts and other "life" situations that knock us off course. The emotional strength to get back up and recalibrate our life takes a sustained and dedicated effort. Isn't the adage "you have to get back on the bike if you want to learn how to ride" something we have all been taught? We cheer the person who has fallen during a race and despite an injury, slowly stands up, wipes the dirt from their bloody knees and continues the race, even though they come in last. The underdog who overcomes adversity is the basis of many Hollywood movies. Isn't this, in a way, seeing the handling of our strongest emotions in an abbreviated amount of time?

Let's look at other definitions by the American Psychological Association. *"Grief is the anguish experienced after significant loss, usually the death of a beloved person ... Grief often includes physiological distress, separation anxiety, confusion, yearning, obsessive dwelling on the past, and apprehension about the future ... Grief may also take the form of regret for something lost, remorse for something done, or sorrow for a mishap to oneself"* (2023).

The terms used to define what the families and friends are going through when someone dies are bereavement and mourning. These are the actions that come from the emotion we call grief, and it can all become confusing when other forms of grief are present, such as disenfranchised grief which may become displaced and ignored.

Disenfranchised grief is defined as "grief that society limits…or may not allow a person to express … examples are grief of parents for still born babies, of teachers for the death of students, and of nurses for the death of patients" (American Psychological Association, 2023).

Notice how the definitions expand beyond the loss of a loved one. So often, we are just busy living our lives. And then, without realizing it, we are fully in the clutches of strong emotions that we may be ill equipped to manage effectively. When any kind of grief, disenfranchised or not, becomes displaced or ignored, the symptoms manifest in other forms of behavior, and you may not make the connection that you are grieving.

For example: We are a few dollars short one week and wonder how we blew through two weeks of funds in such a brief period. We can blame inflation, the increases in consumer goods, but it doesn't help us now when we don't have the cash to pay for something. Sure, we could do without. But don't we go to our default by pulling out a credit card and start using it as a backup to cover normal living expenses? After a few months, we realize that the credit card debt has piled up, and there doesn't seem to be a path to pay it back.

The following is Karel's story to illustrate this point:

KAREL'S STORY

In 1997 we built our dream house in Blue Springs, Missouri. I was a successful real estate Broker Manager, Chairperson of the local Chamber of Commerce, and was fully embedded in the success of our community. In 1998, my husband Rick endured a major skin cancer surgery that could have been physically debilitating. He recovered quickly and returned to work. Five months later, Rick's company eliminated his sales territory, and his pension was threatened if we didn't move to Waterloo, Iowa. All our personal plans crashed and burned. We packed up, moved to a home that was half the size of our dream home because housing inventory was scarce.

This was a crushing move, emotionally and financially. I had to start my real estate career all over again in a community that knew nothing about me. Ground zero and back to basics. After the first year there, I was substantially in debt because my sales were dismal. Frustration, anger, and confusion all roiled inside me as I continually grieved not being in Blue Springs, MO. I remember sitting on my front step extremely depressed and on the verge of tears when Rick settled down beside me and asked, "How are you going to help people learn who you are since you didn't grow up here?" The look on his face did not hold judgement. He was making a simple statement to remind me that I had options. Huh.

In the next week, I designed a program targeted to For Sale by Owner opportunities and a marketing newspaper campaign where people saw pictures of me as I grew up year by year with funny captions. With an incredibly supportive brokerage and management staff, they also helped me research alternative ways to make an income. In one year, my real estate sales production was in the top 5% of real estate agents within my market.

Does this type of grief, frustration, regret, shame, or remorse resonate with you? It's time to consider and evaluate the various stages of grief, both from a clinical point of view and through our storytelling of ourselves and others. Grief is a real emotion that should not go unnoticed. We hope to bring awareness to a subject that is pushed aside because of the stigma associated with feelings that are not recognized as being a part of life challenges.

Chapter 2
Stages of Processing Strong Emotions

When we are trapped in an emotional storm that is ravaging our energy and physical well-being, it's hard to recognize a pattern of how we are cycling through our feelings. In this chapter, we hope to identify not only the clinical approach to managing emotional distress, but to introduce what we have observed over the years.

There are many stages of grief, and there is not one right way to process it. A person experiencing grief will depend on how the person manages difficulties in life. If a person has an avoidance way of coping, then the person may avoid dealing with the feelings to ease the pain of the loss.

Grief work started with Sigmund Freud in 1917 when he wrote about *Mourning and Melancholia* and proposed that a person must do grief work to heal from a loss. Freud's theory did not explain the process associated with grief work (Bialik, 2020). In 1941, Erich Lindemann worked in the psychiatric unit of a hospital in Massachusetts where he did a study that focused on understanding what happened to patients when they had surgery that removed a limb or body part. Lindemann called it "partial death … where the person was now a different person, one without the part. The new person had to rethink how they could relate to a constellation of altered social ties. And they had to figure out what to do with their sorrow" (Rosenfeld, 2018).

Most of Lindemann's work was spent on researching loss, and the deadly fire at Boston's Cocoanut Grove nightclub on November 28, 1942, gave way for him to conduct a historic study of bereavement. Lindemann's work of the Cocoanut Grove fire which took the lives of 492 people and is known as the deadliest nightclub fire where more than 1,000 people were crammed into the building and "would reshape the way the medical world understood grief and redefine the landscape of mental health treatment in the United States" (Rosenfeld, 2018).

It was not until the 1960's when ministers and clinicians would produce the stages of grief as a way of processing feelings. Granger Westberg would use the work of Erich Lindemann to develop what he calls, "Good Grief," to help members of his congregation. Westberg made the information available so that anyone could interpret the stages of grief and did not need a mental health practitioner to explain the process.

Westberg has ten stages of grief: (1962)

Stage One—We are in a state of shock.

"When the sorrow is overwhelming, we are … anesthetized in response to a tragic experience … temporary anesthesia, for it keeps us from having to face grim reality all at once … this shock stage may last a few minutes, few hours, few days … or can go on for some weeks." If the state of shock prolongs for longer period, seek professional help.

Stage Two—We express emotions.

"… begins to dawn upon us how dreadful this loss is … sometimes without warning …wells up within us uncontrollable urge to express grief … allow ourselves to express the emotions we actually feel." Example: little boy falls and skins his knee – "Don't cry!" Child grows up into adulthood and have flashbacks not to cry. "When some great loss is suffered, he cannot cry." Give yourself permission to feel and allow the tears to be your healing balm.

Stage Three—We feel depressed and very lonely.

"Eventually there comes a feeling of utter depression and isolation …we are sure that no one else has ever grieved as we are grieving … no two people face the same kind of loss in the same way…when we find ourselves in the depth of despair…we should remind ourselves…that such depression is normal and a part of good healthy grief … dark days don't last forever." Depression is very real, and it needs to be dealt with through spiritual or clinical counseling.

Stage Four—We may experience physical symptoms of distress.

"…seeing the doctor with a physical complaint … great loss sustained during the past months or year … they have not yet worked through some of the central problems related to the loss … stronger relationship between the illness and the handling of the loss." An emotional loss can create physical symptoms. With a physical hurt, you can see the body healing, unlike an emotional hurt—you can't see the healing. Understanding the symptoms of grief will help you to start connecting to your emotions. Talk therapy is helpful to express your feelings.

Stage Five—We may become panicky.

"… becoming panicky … can think of nothing but the loss…hinders our effectiveness in anything we are trying to do." Fear of the unknown will prevent us from moving forward. What will life be like without the person, job, income, home, and how are you to make it through the next day—one step at a time will help you to face a new reality and a new life. Express your thoughts and feelings about the loss.

Stage Six—We feel a sense of guilt about the loss.

Feelings of guilt of not being there for the person when he or she was alive or leaving a person's bedside in the hospital to get something to eat and upon returning, learning the person died. "Unresolved guilt and misunderstood emotions…can make us miserable for years, or they might come out in a variety of physical symptoms of distress." Don't be afraid to talk about the feelings of guilt with someone who is willing to listen and help but who doesn't feel compelled to evaluate your condition as "bad" or "wrong."

Stage Seven—We are filled with anger and resentment.

"… anger and resentment are a part of 'good grief'" Anger is a healthy emotion that when expressed in a healthy manner can move the person to healing. When anger becomes unhealthy and revengeful, it is important to seek help.

Stage Eight—We resist returning.

"When we attempt to get back into life again, it is much too painful. We would rather grieve than fight the battle of coping with new situations." The landscape of life has changed, and the expectations of a new beginning are uncertain. Life does go on and when you are ready take one step forward, and the next step will become easier.

Stage Nine—Gradually hope comes through.

Glimpse of hope will break through the dark clouds letting the "rays of light to come through." No two people are alike nor grieve alike. Getting to this stage by allowing hope to come through will depend on the person moving through the stages of grief. It takes time, so give yourself permission to grieve. After every rainstorm, the clouds move away giving way for the sun to shine.

Stage Ten—We struggle to affirm reality.

"When we go through any significant grief experience, we come out of it as different people." We may move back and forth through the stages until we get to a place of acceptance of the new reality. As you grieve you will come to understand that there is hope in loving the person in a different way. Life gets better knowing your loved one lives in your heart.

Following Westberg was Kubler-Ross, a Swiss-American Psychiatrist whose pioneering work on *"Death and Dying,"* published in 1969 where Kubler-Ross said there are five stages of grief. Kubler-Ross five stages of grief are:

Denial

In a state of shock about the loss which is like Westberg's definition of stage one. Denial can come from not wanting to accept the reality. By not accepting events that happened, then you don't have to work through the grief process. When in denial, other behaviors can surface creating more issues.

Anger

The person is feeling frustration, anxiety, and irritation. There is a tenseness in the behavior as the person responds to simple activities in life. Being frustrated at family members, friends, or co-workers. "It is everyone's fault" means the person is not taking ownership for their behavior. The level of emotions increases with anxiety.

Bargaining

The bargaining stage is where the person is trying to find the meaning of what has happened. During this stage, telling one's story about the loss or event is helpful for the person. Encouraging the person to talk can be cathartic.

Depression

This is the stage where support and guidance from loved ones can help the person go through the emotions of being overwhelmed, feeling hostility or helplessness and withdraw from their need to escape from reality.

Acceptance

Acceptance allows people to embrace a new reality in their life, moving on by forming new relationships, and exploring options. Don't be surprised if a person gets to this stage and moves back and forth between the other stages. People grieve differently.

The five stages that Kubler-Ross proposed have become acceptable in the clinical world and used by doctors, clinicians, clergies, and lay-people. Westberg's definition of the stages are longer and more definitive than Kubler-Ross, but either one works if it resonates with you.

As we look at the stages of grief, the steps are in an order that seems logical. But life isn't logical! We might accept something, but we are so angry about the situation we cannot see straight. What if we considered the stages of grief as fluid in such a way that our emotions can be acknowledged at any stage of the process? And once we have identified and acknowledged where we are in the process, we can continue to strengthen our resolve and heal.

The stages of grief are different for everyone since a person can move through the stages in what appears to be a haphazard order. Sometimes, you would hear someone say, "I have accepted the death," when it was just a few days or months ago. A person can move from denial to depression without going through the anger or bargaining stage. Everyone is different and understanding the emotions will help towards the healing process.

Below are different ways to look at strong emotions and healing steps:

- Doubting Ourselves through Confusion and Uncertainty
- Rationalizing and Living in a "What If" Reality
- Regret, Shame, Resistance and Denial
- Frustration and Helplessness
- Shame
- Hoarding
- Guilt
- Fear & Panic Evolving into a Perspective Shift
- Reality Check

- Logically Exploring Options
- Resolution and Enacting a New Normal

Let's review each of these steps so there is clarity as to the meaning and application towards working through the grief process. Remember, grief is more than losing a loved one. Loss happens all the time in our lives. It is recognizing what is happening that allows us to start the process of healing.

DOUBTING OURSELVES THROUGH CONFUSION AND UNCERTAINTY

There is nothing more unsettling than not being sure if we are on solid ground in our relationships or in realizing our career and financial goals. Often, others have a way of creating tsunamis of doubt as we struggle to hang on to our personal esteem.

KAREL'S STORY

My mother, Dolores, was a force of nature. She commanded obedience and order from her five children. Working full-time as a registered nurse, she juggled household responsibilities and kept her expectations fully grounded. As I turned sixteen, I couldn't understand why I wasn't asked out on any dates by the boys in my school. I never attended prom or homecoming dances. I know I dressed nicely, had good teeth and hair. I was slim and smart. I asked my mother one day what she thought was going on, and she said with all the authority in the world, "You will never be pretty, but you have a decent personality. Someone will want you for that."

What the hell?

To add to the confusion, she then located a sponsor and registered me as a contestant for the first Miss Teen Age Iowa completion at age seventeen. After purchasing a lovely floor-length gown, getting my hair done by a professional and fussing over my makeup, she shoved me into the limelight. I thought she said I was ugly! Why on earth would she do this to me? I did the interviews with six judges, walked the stage, and did an interpretive reading for my talent section.

My heart was pounding, fully expecting to be humiliated at a state level, ending up in last place out of thirty-plus young girls. Instead, I was voted as first runner up, which floored me. In the glow of that achievement, I felt beautiful—until one judge came up to talk to me. He congratulated me on placing so high in the competition and then revealed, "You know, you aren't really the best-looking girl, but we liked your personality so much, we felt we had to give you high markings! Way to go, sweetheart."

Branded again by a stranger as inadequate.

I held that confusion between having a positive self-esteem and other people's perceptions for years—until I walked down the wedding isle and saw how beautiful I was in my new husband's eyes. My personal level of uncertainty made me a wounded warrior after being branded as not "acceptable" or "loveable."

Imagine what the war zone of social media is doing not only for our children but continues to haunt us as adults! You know how easy it is for a stranger to shatter a person's self-esteem because of the nasty posts that appear in the daily feed. We question why someone would say something like that. And then the uncertainty and doubt surfaces and we may begin to feel that the comments are validated because this is insight from someone outside our personal sphere of influence.

When we are attacked, suddenly for no reason, emotionally we become confused and may begin to believe a false narrative about our lives and how we are perceived by others. Our mind seems to get stuck in a never-ending negative feedback loop.

A way to deal with this type of assault is to first understand that these comments reflect the sender, not the receiver. The easiest way for others to hurt people is using bullying language online and hurtful rhetoric. The goal they have is to feel "better" or "superior" to those they condemn, when in truth, they have shown the world who they really are, bitter and resentful individuals who choose to tear down rather than build up. They have come to judgement without knowing all the facts and reacted emotionally.

We can choose how we react to those comments by building a strong emotional protective wall based solidly on self-knowledge. But what if what the others are saying is true? The question really is, do you want to change aspects about yourself to gain acceptance by others? This is going to require deep internal reflection as you work to solve the problem and deal with it emotionally.

Rationalizing and Living In a "What If" Reality

When we are in emotional turmoil, a lot of soul searching occurs. We tend to look at painful events, harsh people, and unbearable circumstances through a haze of sadness, shame, or regret. As we begin to rationalize how we contributed to a situation, new puzzle pieces begin to fall into place. But is this awareness based upon truth or a fabrication of a "what if" mentality? Emotions of guilt, regret and shame begin to magnify when mired deep within a personal tragedy.

A few years ago, after doing the closing keynote for a conference, Karel walked out of the convention center doors and prepared to figure out where to go to dinner. A woman approached her and introduced herself. Her dull greying hair clung to her slumped shoulders and the sensation of grief oozed from her. During their conversation, she revealed that at sixty-three, Lydia's thirty-five plus years of marriage had collapsed. That morning her husband had cleared out their bank accounts, packed his things, laid divorce papers on the kitchen table and drove off. His only statement as he closed the door was, "I don't love you anymore." Shell shock would be the only way to describe her emotional state. Lydia stressed she never knew anything was wrong between them. Their routine had never changed and there was no warning.

When Karel asked her what she thought could have led to this extraordinary situation, Lydia declared she had no idea. She knew he was bored since their daily routine had been the same for years. She believed she was so busy, he must have felt lonely, even though he was gainfully employed. She thought maybe if she cooked better, dressed up more and had less to say about how money was spent, he would have stayed. Every little nuance she could think of that would lead to him walking out poured out of her mouth. And with each revelation, she rationalized how that would probably be the reason for why he left. It was clear that Lydia's was making her situation "all her fault." She convinced herself that she was the guilty party and thus magnified her grief exponentially.

What happened to the husband's accountability for his part of the relationship? What about his inability to communicate his feelings or thoughts about their marriage? What had changed in his thought process to cause such an aggressive change and blow up their future together?

If Lydia stays in the rationalization mode, which increases her victimization, her grief will linger and could color every future decision she makes. We have learned that rationalization clouds clarity.

Sometimes a person wants to share their story, but because they are in the public eye, the need for anonymity becomes important. The following story is a powerful one. This is the voice of Jane Doe, a woman who had her life rendered upside down from the fairytale life, and yet rose from the ashes strong and resilient.

JANE'S STORY

Where does one begin when their life, marriage, seems to have turned out to be a complete mess and failure?

My husband left stating he was not happy, in what seemed like a midlife crisis, as he was not happy with anything. I told my immediate family and a friend about his moving out. I just couldn't tell anyone else out of embarrassment.

Then my friend asked, "Don't you realize John is a narcissist?" I found an audio book on healing from a narcissist, and as I listened, there were so many memories resonating and confirming that what I was learning is what I had been experiencing and living with. I was hanging on and waiting for him to come home, to want to be with me. I loved him so much, despite my realizing he didn't really love me. Narcissists cannot truly love, I learned.

Although John was taking time for himself, to contemplate his life with the help of a counselor, it became apparent he wasn't even trying to work on us or whether our marriage was something he wanted anymore. After almost six months of living in limbo, I finally did some investigating and found my suspicion from long before he left was true. He was unfaithful. That was nothing new, but something I had ignored, blocked out and would not allow myself to face the truth about. Only what I learned was "unfaithful" I could have never imagined.

That is when I made the decision to file for divorce. The grieving process on top of trying to process everything I learned, the shame I had been feeling was overwhelming and consumed my every thought, almost every moment of each day. Luckily, I had people who were, and still are, the best support anyone could ask for. People I could let in and see behind the façade I had been putting on for years. Finally, I was open and honest about my marriage and what I was dealing with.

The whole time, I hid my pain from my daughter, never letting her see me cry. I worried she would blame me for the end of our family, that it was my fault her father left. I've never spoken poorly about her father to her or in front of her. I want her to see me as a strong resilient woman, to be an example to her, but I also don't want her to know the truth of things. Again, feeling ashamed and worrying about what she would or will think of me, when she learns the truth behind us no longer being a family.

Through it all, I have rediscovered me . . . the real, fun, and adventurous me. I have let go of shame for the most part although I still struggle today, three years later, with feeling worthy of love, that someone could ever love me. It's still a process, probably will be for some time yet, and I have become okay with that.

I had been given a book called The Art & Power of Acceptance and in it were two pages with statements of what acceptance is and is not. These statements made an impact on me, providing a mind shift in how I was looking at things and has seemed to be part of what helps me move forward. I started doing yoga, which centers around being mindful, taking time to focus on yourself. I learned the importance of setting an intention at the beginning of my practice and at the end releasing, healing, and rejuvenating. I enjoy my fellow yogi's and the "tribe" friends we have become. I keep myself open to new things, getting out of my comfort zone.

Even though it would be nice to have someone to share my life and adventures with, I'm at peace with being alone. I have several friend groups that I do things with each month. I get out of my comfort zone and even do a few things on my own. One of the best things that came out of the end of my marriage was relief. So much stress is gone, no more feeling like a failure and a horrible person. I realized I was becoming a person John didn't like or want anymore, a person I no longer liked anymore either. It wasn't just about me and who I had become. It was about seeing what I had become—a reaction: a reaction to not having trust in my marriage or in him, the lack of respect he had for me, the resentment that had grown in me towards him and the resentment towards myself for who I had become.

So much of what you feel and go through is the same stages of grief as if a loved one passes away, with sadness and anger being the biggest of them, not just anger at the other person or what has happened, but anger with yourself. That is the hardest one to get past, feeling ashamed, pathetic, at fault and foolish.

But then you do come to acceptance and a sort of peace. Sort of, as you are on a journey and like any journey, it has its ups and downs, trials and tribulations. There is also beauty, joy, love, and laughter. You just must keep moving forward, enjoying life, and learning from it all.

Taking a true look at your life and all the contributing factors that caused the moment of pain and loss is a huge step to healing. We must know the facts and accept our complicity in the outcomes. Only then can we begin to rebuild our resolve for a better outlook on life.

DENIAL, REGRET & RESISTANCE

Have you noticed that sometimes situations have a way of magnifying differences between individual perspectives? What initially appears to be an innocent comment made by someone we love somehow escalates into an internal family feud. Parents and siblings take sides as they claim their perspective as righteous. The non-involved family members watch on as it seems nothing can be done to breach the barrier that's been built.

In all honesty, don't we all envision lovely family holiday reunions, you know, like a *Lifetime Channel* movie? We can't wait to experience the smells of home cooking and join in the laughter as everyone watches *A Christmas Story* again for the tenth viewing. However, when the time arrives to celebrate, someone may boycott the gathering or threaten not to come if the "other one" shows up. As a result, family members go through the motions of politeness but underneath runs an ongoing resistance to getting issues out into the open and resolving them.

Out of respect for the feelings of others, we avoid having important conversations. It's perceived that there is great danger in unveiling truths which in turn might heal the hurt that is inflicted on everyone every time the family gathers.

There is nothing worse than when someone from outside the family joins the event and takes you aside and says, "What the hell is going on between you and Emily?"

No one wants to air their dirty laundry to the public, so the false smile surfaces and our response may be, "Oh, she's just tired." We resist acknowledging the pain of the conflict because it, quite frankly, hurts! Denial of the issues seems easier to manage.

Perhaps simple Midwest advice can be considered—let it roll off your back like water does on a duck. It resonates, but it's hard to follow. In its place settles grief because the healing we long for may never come to pass.

Kimberly Kew is an adventurous identical mirror twin raised by World War II First and Second Lieutenant's parents. She proclaims that she is the only member of her family without credentials or various letters of the alphabet following her name except for M.O.M., earned as a stay-at-home mother for her two sons. Most recently, at 60 years of age, she worked as a wrangler at the Roosevelt Corrals in Yellowstone National Park taking guests on horseback guided trail rides through the back county and driving wagons pulled by teams of draft horses to a cookout where over two hundred guests enjoyed an all-you-can-eat steak dinner nightly.

Sounds like a resourceful and strong person, the kind that anyone can rely upon. Here is her story:

KIM'S STORY

Trust me when I say you never in your lifetime want to hear the words Lewy Body Dementia . . . ever. For me, those three words destroyed all plans of sharing my life and adventures with my friend I so loved. This disease quietly seeped into our hopes and dreams. It corrupted trust and vandalized the compassion and love we once shared. It felt like this disease laid in wait for years building emotional turmoil and stealing everything, I thought I knew or felt in my heart.

Once the diagnosis was finally discovered and revealed, I understood with crippling guilt and grief all those reasons why—I had been shielded by the blissfulness of ignorance and truly didn't know what I didn't know. My ignorance was so blatant; I never even knew enough to enjoy the bliss. The worst was yet to come, and yet I gave my friend and partner in life of sixteen years my word we would shoulder this burden of Lewy Body Dementia together. I promised him I would stand with him against all else and walk with him through his darkest symptoms. Ultimately, I was able to fulfill my promise, preserve my word, shelter my vulnerable and trusting friend only and solely because of the help of my family who stepped up, didn't listen to the noise, and did what we all believed was right.

I was grieving because I was blinded by ignorance of all the simple little signs and whispers of this ugly disease. I felt in my heart something was wrong, but I had no understanding why. I recognize now I can't be too comfortable because life will change "just like that." I don't believe you ever "add" just . . . but rather "just" keep walking, or crawling, if need be, for another minute, another hour and learn how to live today. Loss means that the life you once lived and the person you love is gone—no matter if that loss happens in a second or agonizingly slow.

I learned too late time had run out. Today was all I had left. I didn't see it; I didn't even know enough to honor it and my second chance I call tomorrow was going to be unrecognizable and different, different in a way that steals all peace of mind. It's a very harsh lesson to learn we only have today, there is only the here and now with the ones we love. Be selfish and greedy with every moment or opportunity to share in your loved ones being, because someday that, too, will be gone.

I regret not having stepped up by defending my relationship with my loved one, protecting my feelings, and shielding my life as I built it, as we built it, from those who would disrespect, step over boundaries, and invade our personal life as a longtime loving couple. I gave respect to those who neither deserved it nor earned it.

I must believe there is a loving, giving full life out there waiting for me and deserving of my good faith, my goodwill, and my light. I just can't wait too long deciding whether I'm deserving of it. The hospice bereavement information I received was helpful in recognizing how those left behind grieve, but I have been given little in the way of tools in which to help me rebuild from this crippling storm of grief. I understand I am alone on this path, but I do feel cradled by those who know me best and who love me most and whom I call family. I will always be especially grateful to my two sister lions for their love, for their courage and for their voice throughout this journey filled with grace and love.

Working through regret, resistance and denial is absolutely one of the toughest emotional efforts we face. The power of seeking help and developing a forward-looking outlook on your life takes time, but the result can bring you solace and hopefully resolution to your rage or regret. The toughest lesson we have had to learn is "life is not fair." Over time and with dedicated self-analysis, we do begin to understand that it's what we do with our new insight that counts.

SHAME

Shame and guilt are two different emotions. According to Keller, *"Guilt is the feeling that you have done something bad. Shame is the feeling that you are bad. Guilt relates to your behaviors. Shame connects with your very identity. Guilt is common and normative emotion experienced by grievers"* (2022). During the grieving process, grievers will consume themselves with the "should have," "could have," and/or "would have" thought patterns. However, these patterns are not healthy and can lead to unhealthy and unwanted behaviors.

Your work environment or social media can bring out our insecurities and may make us subject to passive aggressive behavior or cause us to develop overwhelming feelings of being unappreciated or overlooked. If you read the headlines today, we have developed a cancel culture where individuals and social media groups actively engage in public shunning and seeking retribution. This may cause us to keep our heads down, don't cause any disruption and hope things get better, which in turn erodes at our sense of self-worth.

The emotions relating to shame are so powerful, it can lead to self-harm. We can lose perspective of who and what we stand for. We realign what priorities are paramount—which might be something we had lost sight of. We can internalize strong emotions of regret, remorse, indignation, and rage that all surface because of our feelings of worthlessness.

We become unlovable in our own minds. And that is the tragedy that leads to a downward spiral.

In the 2022 Hulu series *The Act*, a character tells another "Sometimes the only thing to do is to walk through the fire to the other side." This is a vivid description of survival—taking all the beatings and slung arrows as they come. It will end in some manner, and maybe not as well as we might wish. But it will end, and once you walk through the fire, at the very least you know you can do it. Hopefully, you don't just survive it. You're stronger and better for the experience.

The story becomes one of personal redemption. What are you willing to do to love yourself once again? By acknowledging the cause of the shame and then taking steps to mitigate the damage done, we at least feel empowered. Is this easy? Absolutely not—but necessary to self-redemption.

HOARDING

Hoarding is an interesting manifestation of how some people manage strong emotions. These individuals accumulate "stuff" and establish an emotional attachment to every item either because they perceive it to be valuable or connected to a special event or person. There is a difference between hoarding and collecting.

According to Browne, "hoarding is when a person has difficulty getting rid of items because they feel a strong need to keep them. They may feel distressed if they must discard them. The ongoing buildup of collected items can lead to unsafe and unhealthy living spaces. It can also cause tension in personal relationships and severely diminish the quality of daily life" (2020).

At some point, hoarding can become so severe that it's beyond the person's ability to handle it themselves. The support provided must be constructive and not be done in such a manner to make the hoarding person become defensive (Browne, 2020).

If you find yourself compulsively keeping objects and it is interfering with your quality of life, seek help before you compromise your personal health and safety. Ask yourself "how did I get here? How did I lose control of all that is accumulating around me?" The underlying issues may stem back to childhood or a specific loss or event. Regardless of the cause, being aware of your circumstance and getting help is the first step to healing (Browne, 2020).

GUILT

Being driven by guilt is a strong motivator. We may feel we were the cause or source of a problem and live our lives trying to make up for our shortcomings. These feelings of guilt can filter every ambition and sense of purpose we have without us ever realizing it. The next story was shared during the last few days of Donna's life. The heave burden of guilt weighed on her for seventy-five years and framed decisions she made for her entire adult life.

DONNA'S STORY

Donna, born in 1924, was the oldest daughter of six children. Around the age of 10, her mother became very ill and bedridden after delivering a baby boy named Georgie. Georgie was a "blue baby" because he suffered from a bad heart. He wailed continually throughout the day and night, unable to breathe well. Georgie suffered because medical options during the Great Depression were limited.

Her mother looked to Donna to take care of all the needs of the family. This meant making the meals, cleaning the house, babysitting all the younger siblings, helping her mother as she lay in bed and anything else her mother would have normally done around the house.

Georgie continued to shriek, a pounding incessant sound that invaded her every moment at home. Donna cradled Georgie in her arms at night, hoping he would fall asleep, but that happened rarely. With no sleep, hard heavy work taking care of the family, schoolwork and an infant that was in distress, she became despondent.

Exhausted after several months, showing dark shadows under her eyes, and losing weight, she suffered alone. Her teachers knew what was happening but could do nothing to intervene. These were harsh times for everyone.

One exceptionally bad night, Donna prayed to God, asking for relief from the baby's crying. She begged God to help her as she stroked the wailing baby in her arms.

The following day, after school, Donna came home to see the limp body of Georgie wrapped in a shroud on the kitchen table. Donna remembers stopping in the doorway and hearing the silence. And to her mortification, her first thought was "God answered my prayers."

Upon touching her small fragile brother on the table, she doubled over in grief and guilt from the feeling she had caused Georgie's death. Unable to forgive herself for the horror of a young life lost, Donna made a commitment for her future career: to become a nurse and never let another small life end if she could help it.

Through unspeakable odds, financial difficulties, and harsh recriminations from her parents for her choice of becoming a nurse, Donna survived the grueling educational standards, and graduated as a Registered Nurse (RN) at age 21. She then joined the US Army Nurse Corp in 1945, serving during WWII.

Donna married and raised a large family. She lived up to her promise and served as a staff nurse, nursing home administrator and instructor for a local community college until she retired.

On her death bed, she shared this story with me and hoped that her guilt from her wish seventy-plus years before had been wiped clean.

In this story, you can understand why a person might have an undercurrent sadness. Reactions to situations or people may be a direct result of deep guilt they are trying to resolve. Let her story become a powerful catalyst for you in terms of learning how to release guilt. We must understand that often our drives and passion have a reason. Once we identify the source, then we can determine our ultimate outcomes. Let's not take a lifetime to find peace. Give yourself permission to release guilt and build something positive for your life.

FRUSTRATION AND HELPLESSNESS

Unresolved problems and the inability to "fix it" is the perfect nesting ground to grow doubt and a prevailing sense of inadequacy in our abilities to make the world "right." A classic example is shouting at the cable news station as our elected officials tilt too far to one extreme or another. All we have is one vote and the rest is completely out of our hands individually.

Frustration is an angry word, and it chews unrelentingly at our self-esteem and sense of purpose.

KAREL'S STORY

I believe every parent wants to be a good one. When that precious being is placed in your arms, something profound happens, a love and connection that is incredibly strong, almost breathtaking. When raising a family, Rick and I had to figure things out on the fly. What promotional opportunities do we take advantage of and how do they secure our family financially? As a result, we relocated four times before our son reached fourth grade.

We were a tight unit. Home was wherever we ended up. As a result, our son became very independent. Extremely smart, quick to learn new things and always exploring how far he could push the boundaries, he seemed to thrive. Several moves meant new schools and friends. Rick and I felt excited with the new opportunities, but looking back, we know our son must have grieved leaving his support system behind. I'll never forget seeing him wave out the back window of the car as we left Pittsburgh, his best friend standing forlornly in the driveway.

Each location had different school expectations and cultures, from big town Minneapolis to small town Mankato, from Mankato back to the big town of Pittsburgh and then rerouting to Blue Springs, Missouri outside of Kansas City. For the first three cities, our son thrived in Talented and Gifted programming. Then the brakes came on with our final move. Our son learned that "being smart" didn't make good friends, so he dropped out of the classes he loved. His grief manifested itself in frustration at moving so often, and fighting his helplessness at not being able to do anything about it provided the catalyst for rebellion.

As parents, we couldn't understand what was happening. By sixteen, we were at a loss as to what to do to find balance. It then clicked as I read a sentence to my husband from a novel that went "God doesn't give us the child we want. He gives us the child we need."

We finally understood we were dealing with our son's grief and our son's sense of instability. Once our perspective changed, behaviors and attitudes shifted.

The underlying regret and frustration, as illustrated in this story, can evolve over time, gnawing at our emotions like a scavenging rat. But imagine if tragedy strikes repeatedly to the same person. Often, it magnifies the impact of the loss they experience. The following is a very personal story that may hit home for you. Reading how Fred has survived his personal catastrophe will provide you with perspective and hope.

Dr. Fredrick G. Buehler, Jr. has been in the real estate business for more than twenty years as a multi-million-dollar producer, manager, Broker of Record, educator and now director of the area's preeminent real estate schools. He earned his Doctor of Philosophy in Real Estate Management, Doctor of

Philosophy in Metaphysical Psychology and Juris Doctor in law. He also hosts a nationally syndicated radio show called *Straight Talkin' Real Estate* with a weekly audience in the thousands.

FREDRICK'S STORY

My personal crisis or tragedy occurred March 2020, when the entire world went into lockdown over the COVID-19 crisis. I feared for my parents, who are older, that they would somehow be affected by this. I was teaching a class just before we were ordered to stay home, and I explained to the class that I was concerned about my parents. Something I wished I never said out loud to the universe. I don't know what it was, but something just told me this wasn't gonna be good.

My parents were planning their 50th wedding vows renewal. They had been trying to get their marriage excepted by the Catholic Church for fifty-one years. They were married legitimately in another church, but being devout Catholics, this was important for them to be recognized by the Catholic Church. Particularly my mom. They were planning a small service on February 15. Mom wasn't feeling so good, but she was happy that this was finally going to happen. In fact, I had never seen her so happy.

My mother had a very difficult life growing up as an orphan child. Her parents died when she was very young in a car accident. So most of our life she spent not always seeming to be happy. This time, though, she smiled and smiled and smiled. A few days after the service I called to find out how they were doing. Things seem to be OK. We texted back-and-forth mostly, but then the weekend after, text messaging sort of slowed down. She said she wasn't feeling good and then some point after she was complaining about not being able to fully breathe. The text messages stopped. No reply to my messages, which wasn't unusual from time to time. Out of concern, of course, I called and left messages. No response. At this point, I then reached out to my father. He said that Mom needed to go to the hospital. He dropped her off, then called all three of his sons to let us know.

Things escalated from there quickly. My dad was not able to stay, and we were told that Mom had tested positive for Covid. He also tested positive for Covid although he was not experiencing symptoms. Mom, however, was being placed on a ventilator. This went on for over a week; it was all a blur. We received calls telling us she was getting better and then not getting better. They were doing everything they could for her. Then finally we received the phone call that her organs and body systems were shutting down. Shortly afterwards, my father told us mom had passed.

It's very hard to describe that particular moment. I wasn't sure if I was feeling anything but numbness and utter concern for my father. I've never heard him in that state before. He was always strong-willed and held his composure most of the time. But this time it wasn't the same. The woman that he has been with for over fifty-five years was gone.

As far as how I handled it, well, let's just put it this way I didn't. I exploded into crying hysterically. I felt as though my heart, my very existence, my soul had all been ripped out of my body. I did manage to compose myself, and then I quickly went into survival mode, checking on my brothers and my father to make sure everyone was OK.

The big problem here was that we were not able to see her. We couldn't go over to my father's house to be with him to comfort each other. We were in lockdown and all we had was a telephone. The process of trying to figure out what just happened was overwhelming. Fear, despair, hopelessness, and anger were the emotions that would just repeat themselves in a cycle over and over and over and over. It was like a hamster wheel that just wouldn't stop.

At first, I wasn't sure what I was grieving over. The shock of losing our mother out of nowhere was something that was out of our control was increased by the fact that we couldn't see her off. We couldn't even go to the hospital to say our goodbyes. It wasn't until a week at least before reality set in. At this point, we needed to start planning for a funeral. That's when the true grieving started when the gravity of the situation sunk in and made us emotionally understand that she wasn't coming back.

At the same time my business at the school was online. We immediately had to figure out how to shift to meet the demands of the students that signed up for school. I had 120 students that semester waiting to complete their education. I had to find strength to pull myself together to provide that educational experience the students were expecting and needed. Honestly, as the world was shutting down, I was really blessed that the school was doing so well. In fact, it continued month after month after month. That is truly what kept me going.

I knew this was never going to be normal ever again. Trying to recalibrate was nothing short of difficult. I tried several methods of meditation to clear my thoughts, thinking of the memories and all the positive times she was available in my life. Feeling grateful—all those things that I would normally do to deal with grief—were just not working. I couldn't find peace with this. I did seek counseling, which was at first difficult to get an appointment. But to this day, I still see a counselor twice a month.

This tragedy was about to take a turn for the worse. This whole time during the lockdown from Covid, my father was not able to get to his doctor appointments. He's been battling lung and prostate cancer and was in remission for many years. This very short time that he was not able to get to the doctors would prove to be deadly. As it turns out the cancer in his lungs, the spots, were growing fast and very aggressively.

By November 2020 after finally being able to get to the doctor, he was notified that he only had a few months to live. The cancer spread quickly throughout his body and spine. He was given an option to receive heavy doses of chemo and radiation with a very low percentage of survival. The risk was that it would burn him out or the cancer would kill him. He chose the treatments. My dad never told us that they only gave him a few months to live. He wanted to fight this thing! He didn't want to give up or show his weakness.

My brother and I stepped away from our families to move in with dad to care for him. Our youngest brother couldn't do much because he lived one state over, and he was dealing with even more tragedy himself. His wife passed away at the age of 32, a month after mom passed, leaving him with his only child to care for. So, it was up to myself and my middle brother to handle things. As his continual caretakers, we watched Dad decline quickly, staying night and day for weeks, rotating our schedules. We spent Thanksgiving back-and-forth, Christmas back-and-forth. Nothing was working well, and he continued to decline. Dad was admitted to a hospital because of his decline, and eventually was able to be discharged to a rehab center. When we finally brought him home, he was in the care of Hospice.

It wasn't even 10 months since Mom died, and then Dad died April 2, 2021. Did he die from a broken heart? Possibly. Or did cancer just defeat him? Dad fought hard, but it wasn't enough. For us, the back-to-back loss was insurmountable. To this day I just can't believe it.

When I look back at regrets and think about whether I did something that I shouldn't have or whether I could have done something different, I don't think so. I honestly had a good relationship with my parents. I'd call them weekly, tell them that I loved them when I saw them, and I would always hug them. They *didn't always reciprocate, and I didn't get in return the same warm and fuzzy feelings that I was giving them. But I knew them well and accepted it.*

The one thing that I personally regret (and probably why I'm having trouble and struggling through this) is that with my father, we were able to see him off. In fact, I held his hand as he took his last breath. With mom, we didn't get to be with her. The last time we met was at her wedding. She was smiling. She was happy. Those memories are what I have and that's a good thing. But there's this thing about funerals and seeing them off—I didn't have a chance with mom.

My behavior has modified a little bit since the passing of both of them. I've slowed down in my thinking and taken more time to listen to others and being more in the moment. I hope for a sign from them (mom and dad) and spend time planning a bit more for the inevitable. I'm trying to accept the fact that we are all going to die.

I try to live my life interacting with people more like how my parents did. They were givers— they helped people—they were involved in the community. In fact, they were known as Mr. and Mrs. Santa Claus. Christmas was my mom's thing. They brought joy and happiness to thousands of children in our region. Many of these people reached out to share their condolences and their memories of Mr. and Mrs. Santa Claus. Hearing those stories truly makes me happy. They did what they did, and that's who they were.

So, what do I do now? How do I continue? How do I address my feelings? The impact of the legacy they left, one of giving, serving and really being available to help others in need, feels like something I do already. The difference for me now is I'm scaling up my "giving," both financially and dedicating time to help others. I continue therapy, it helps. Talking about them, celebrating them constantly, thinking about them and remembering more of the good times than the bad times and visiting the gravesite all help. But it's the act of helping others that helps me best cope and deal with this new way of life.

Imagine the loss Fred feels in his life. His journey through his emotional turmoil is taking him to a place of community and refocusing his energy to healing not only himself, but others.

FEAR AND PANIC EVOLVING INTO A PERSPECTIVE SHIFT

Counselors and mentors for years have declared that the darkest hour is before dawn; that everything will be resolved with the clarity of the morning sun. Sounds delightful, but what are we to do in those dark hours that harbor fear of the unrelenting reality we are faced with, an upcoming event, ongoing abuse, or a realization that we have decided that others might not accept us or the decisions we have made?

Panic can set in if we let it. As we tally up our failures and shortcomings, we also face honestly our deepest fears. When we survive the night, we begin to understand we can only control *our* response to a problem or situation. We come to the realization that we can do better, deserve better and begin to set a new course for living.

KAREL'S STORY

May of 2022, I spent twenty-five days in the hospital. Early on the morning of May 19th, I underwent a procedure to scope my stomach. The doctor ended up removing a large gall stone that had embedded itself in my bile duct. Released at noon, I returned to the emergency room at 2:00 PM, doubled over in excruciating pain. Diagnosed with pancreatitis, massive amounts of fluids were pumped into my system and physicians prescribed Fentanyl as they tried to keep my pain under control. Over the next twelve hours, my blood pressure soared, my heart started missing beats, kidneys and liver became compromised, and I had trouble breathing as fluid filled my lungs. As one nurse put it, "You were in such a dire condition, we were very worried you wouldn't make it." I don't remember much of the first four days, which in retrospect is a blessing.

Because of the fluids, I gained forty-five pounds in five days. Swollen beyond belief, I looked nine months pregnant with bulging legs, fingers, and arms. We then had the problem of getting that water weight off, and I developed pneumonia. After ten days of being bedridden, poked, and prodded, and enduring multiple blood draws (three or four a day), I realized I could barely walk, lift my arms, or sit up in a chair for more than fifteen minutes.

The doctors then worked to eliminate the fluid by pumping Lasik into me. That's a high-grade diuretic, and it is hard on your body.

I spent fifteen days in the medical section of the hospital, then transferred to physical therapy. It took ten days before I would pass the physical therapist tests that enabled me to be released home. By then, I had lost all the water weight and then some, a total of fifty-five pounds. I looked and felt so fragile. Now I know what the term skin and bones mean.

During those twenty-five days, I couldn't believe how I went from being healthy and active to potentially being put into a nursing home because I couldn't care for myself. It happened so quickly! I remember lying in bed, trying to regain who I was. I asked Rick not to tell anyone I was in the hospital, other than close family, because I've never been witnessed as being so weak. I'm the strong one. I'm the one that takes care of other people. And now I'm possibly looking at being dependent upon other people for the rest of my life?

I admit, in the dark, when Rick went home after sitting with me for thirteen hours, I tried not to panic. Fear of losing my vitality and becoming disabled for life started to eat away at my ability to rebound. I found it hard to sleep because I felt my life was slipping out of my control. I'm so grateful to my friend Kathy McCarty who showed up, unannounced three times, to see how I was doing. She wanted to keep me in touch with the outside world. I didn't know how much I needed her to help quell my panic until I saw her. Reflected in her eyes, I could see the concern she had over my situation. But then, she did something magical—she gave me a goal and refused to let me give up.

Kathy and I had a trip planned for mid-July. She told me not to count myself out but to work to get better so we could tour those grand homes in Newport, Rhode Island as planned. From that moment, I determined to do one more thing… take 20 more steps… sit up ten minutes longer…just go a bit further every day. It became my mantra—focus on where I could be if I applied myself. No one could help me but me.

We did have to cancel the trip because my energy level was still too low. But by the end of September, I was back to walking two miles a day and lifting weights.

This experience shifted my perspective considerably. Before this incident, tasks, goals, and objectives dictated my daily routine. There were lists to follow, things to do and people to meet. Achievement overruled enjoying the moment fully. Now, recognizing that life can change at a snap of the fingers, each moment is precious to me. I'm noticing the nuances of my relationships, observing situations with a non-judgmental eye, and seeking only to engage in a manner that is positive and life affirming.

When we survive a catastrophic event, we grow to understand we can't control everything. Isn't it said that when we plan, God laughs? We begin to understand that more intimately than ever before. The true gift we can embrace is accepting fully our time living and breathing. We don't have time for lamenting about what was or what could have been. We can accept our limitations, ask for help when we need it and feel grateful for being able to do what we can. Living with no regrets—how beautiful is that?

Reality Check

Facing the truth is something many of us don't like to do. It's like studying ourselves under the harshest bathroom light and seeing every wrinkle and facial flaw as we age. The ears are getting bigger, nose a bit longer, and the fresh smooth skin is now a thing of the past. When the hell did the age spots appear? We realize we look like our parents and have no idea how we got there without noticing. Reality checks occur aggressively, which in turn requires us to stop, reflect and make new plans that may not be wanted, but necessary.

Mark Barker, owner of Career Education Systems in the Kansas City area and an accomplished real estate instructor, suffered through an unwanted divorce. He learned that what we want sometimes isn't ours to keep. As a result of the divorce, he lost his home, family, and 50 percent of his income for the next twenty-five years.

We can't imagine the pain a person must feel, a sense of abandonment, frustration by not being able to "fix it," and the sense of being blindsided. Mark learned that love is not enough. When a person marries, he feels we must be prepared to accept the worst and hope and pray it doesn't happen. Mark also believes we should never walk away without fighting for what we love. His biggest regret was not fighting harder for his children rather than "compromise" for the sake of the kids.

A huge lesson learned—we will never regret fighting for love even if we lose it.

As a very stoic person, Mark presents a highly professional image to the public. Don't we all have that tendency—never let them see us sweat? Mark knew, at that time, he was grieving because his emotions were running rampant. He recognized that what was happening in his marriage was diametrically opposed to what he believed was right. Again, he was gaining clarity through a personal reality check. Once he recognized this, he sought professional counselling for two years, reaffirmed his Christian faith, and joined Arthur Murray dance classes to restart his "non-work" life. He was affirming life and developing options.

After an expanded period of recovery, Mark began dating his future second wife for two years. By accepting the fact that we can do everything that we believe is "right" and it still may not work, he became more of a "giver" to others. And for that, many have benefited from his insight and realignment of personal purpose.

Reality checks are painful, no matter how you look at them. What "was" suddenly "isn't" anymore and you have to adapt. The following illustrates this poignantly. Cindy Chandler lives a life dedicated to her family, community and profession serving as a North Carolina Real Estate Commissioner and real estate educator. She is a living testament to personal resilience. Here is her story:

CINDY'S STORY

I've always had an excellent memory and razor focus. That's how I've been so productive. I could never figure out why people were so inefficient! My condition was somewhat OCD, but it served me well. However, my brain never quite shut off. Medication helped, but it was hard to be me when I was on it. I could write all night and complete things without interruption. I despised having my schedule upset and rarely had to change things. I was always the reliable one. That's what I was used to being.

Let's rewind to seven years ago... both my healthy parents died within three weeks of each other with no warning. I, as an only child, had to learn how to go with the flow. I learned that the world did not stop because I had to change my schedule, recognizing sometimes there were good reasons to alter my plans.

My mantra regarding change became "NO BIG DEAL." Wow! I became easier to be around and much more flexible with others and, to be honest, a bit with myself.

In November 2020, I became extremely ill due to Covid. I've never been seriously sick or injured before and had never been treated in a hospital emergency room. For three weeks, languishing in bed with a 103 fever, I struggled to breathe, which in turn forced me onto oxygen. I could crawl to the bathroom, but that was it. When I could finally sit up and concentrate, I saw 2,500 unanswered emails. The impact of what I had endured almost overwhelmed my husband, who was terrified that I would die. It took me months to recover physically, not ever reaching 100 percent. Even though I was confused over my lesser abilities, I was grateful to be alive. I became empathetic to others who had experienced being seriously ill.

In 2022, my husband was hospitalized five times in five months. This meant concentrating on family and readjusting my work life. Reinforced by my new perception about life and maintaining schedules, I acknowledged it wasn't the end of the world to reschedule a class. The experience fundamentally altered my perspective on adaptability. Yes, I want to keep all my commitments! But if a family member is in crisis, all bets are off.

During this period, I started feeling off balance and endured brain surgery for trigeminal neuralgia. Funny thing was, I wasn't concerned and referred to it as a "minor procedure." Minor? A surgeon cut a hole into my skull and operated along my brain stem as I lay trapped in a halo. There was no real pain from the operation except for a bit of discomfort on the scalp. When I woke up, I realized they shaved off some of my hair! Really! That was what I was worried about? My hair? Strange what we focus on during traumatic times.

It's been six months now and the residual effects included positive and negative results. My face pain is gone but I have lost my ability to focus. Today, I've little sense of urgency and can be easily distracted which results in my finding things partially done around the house. I've finally realized this is my new normal. It took me a bit to understand what was going on, and I've had to reinforce myself emotionally. My physician feels it might improve in the next six months. But this might be the way I will be from this point forward.

Wow! For sixty-five years I was OCD and had laser focus as well as an incredible memory, which allowed me to get a lot done in a short period of time. Before all of this, I was the most efficient person anyone knew. Now, I think I'm average in those areas and adapting to this reality. Quite frankly, it's much easier to live. I'm much more accepting of others. I'm more content overall which in turn allows my brain to get plenty of rest. I've experienced a personal perception shift that is different in a big way.

The lesson from this experience: Play the cards you are dealt. I'd rather be less "sharp" and have no excruciating pain in my face. If previous abilities and tendencies return, I can deal with it now more effectively. If they don't, I'm OK. It's all good.

LOGICALLY EXPLORING OPTIONS

Earlier we used the analogy that being overwhelmed with emotions seems like we are in a deep dark hole lined with slick walls. No way to get a firm grip and climb our way out. There is no way we can say what works for one person will work for another. Our upbringing, parental guidance and experiences all shape how we deal with adversity. And let's face it, managing strong emotions and grief is an adversity.

At this point, we feel it's important to address the inner child in all of us. Some of us are fortunate to have been raised by parents who taught us to be independent thinkers. These engaged parents spent time explaining that every decision comes with a variety of options. If we explore the pros and cons fully and understand the logical outcome of any decisions made, we are well on our way to self-reliance.

Others of us are wounded warriors. We became independent by default because our parents had long working hours, displayed lack of interest or succumbed to addiction—the reasons are numerous. What results is a child left to their own devices, relying upon the kindness of strangers and their own internal fortitude. Often, children end up in the reverse role of becoming the parent, making decisions beyond what we might expect a child to address. Just writing this is painful, and as a community we grieve for these types of situations.

When we are mired in trauma, it can be impossible to see what options exist. We are too busy trying to survive. Stories abound of women going back to marriages where they know their spouse will continue to beat them. We shout that there are women shelters, community services, churches or authorities that can help them. But if we are buried deep in fear, panic, grief in our circumstances, how on earth can we reach up and do something for ourselves? It must be like an emotional quicksand. Our only savior is someone who reaches an arm or branch from solid ground and pulls us out.

Somewhere along the line, we must stop and breathe.

Just stop.

Evaluate your surroundings and relationships devoid of emotional shading. How would someone outside of the situation see this? Taking time to gain clarity is the first step to uncovering options.

Resolution and Enacting a New Normal

Where does "grit" come from? Is it something we are born with? Why do some people tackle adversity energetically and others succumb to it under an overwhelming feeling of helplessness? The Cleveland Clinic calls this the "acceptance" stage. People see what has happened and acknowledge its impact, emotionally, physically, and financially.

Personally, "resolve" is what we have seen people do when suffering from an extreme event. It's almost like they play defense by recalibrating their internal strength and then use their newfound power to create something new. We have seen others reclaim their sense of purpose, choosing to go on offense rather than being at the mercy of fate.

Missy Layfield, along with her husband Bob, owned *The Island Sand Paper* which covered news in Fort Myers Beach and adjacent areas. Her ability to take on life challenges is something to behold. Here is her story:

Missy's Story

In late September 2022, we lost our Florida home to Hurricane Ian. While the cement block shell still stood, everything inside was ruined due to 7 feet of toxic storm surge in the house. This had been our primary home for over a dozen years. The community it stood in was our community, our friends. Ian also took the lives of several members of our community, whom we knew.

After the pandemic caused our sudden retirement two years before, we were planning to spend the next ten years enjoying retirement in our beach community. Ian ended that possibility. Worse, the decision wasn't as clear cut as we expected. We knew we wouldn't be able to rebuild the house due to building codes and our inability to do the work ourselves; insurance companies didn't give any guidance, just small offers that didn't *allow repair or rebuilding. We struggled for over three months, wrestling with the grief of so much loss and decisions about what to do next. Build, sell, build, sell? With what and how and where? Nothing was clear; nothing was easy.*

The indecision created was nerve-wracking. At the two-month post-storm marker, I recognized that I wasn't shaking off the extreme sadness and feelings of loss from the storm aftermath. I cried several times a week when thinking of someone or something lost forever.

We began talking about what we could do ourselves, taking our destiny into our own hands since waiting for the insurance companies was creating more stress and anxiety in our lives. We tore down the destroyed house and bought another one in a new community. I sought professional help, but what made the biggest difference was, we made the conscious decision to focus on forward rather than back, while keeping in touch with friends in our beach community.

In retrospect, I regret not reaching out for help sooner. A lifetime of being the one who kept it together in a crisis did not prepare me to deal with this level of loss/grief. Talking more with others who shared my hurricane loss grief would have helped also. Knowing that others were struggling with the same sadness might have helped lessen the emotional impact a bit.

Today, I'm purposefully focusing on positive and happy thoughts, what I'm grateful for, as well as trying to exercise more.

I am getting help for the ongoing anxiety and depression as well as talking and listening to other survivors. I'm collecting items to create a memorial of our lives in our beach community for our new home.

Missy's natural resilience and ability to focus on a new purpose is helping her transition into her new life. Will echoes of the pain still creep in? Of course. But she understands intellectually and emotionally her life has changed and this shift in her life was beyond her control. Concentrating on integrating into her new community may provide her with perspective and wellbeing. For Missy and her family, reestablishing their family in a new location will bring new opportunities and experiences. And she is ready with an open heart and arms.

Another arena that is a natural reservoir for sadness, desperation and adaptability is the world of a caregiver. Monica Neubauer is a Maverick Motivator. Her mission is to help people grow in positive directions in their personal and professional lives. She is the author of *Straight Talk for Real Estate Success: 80 Tips for Structuring, Organizing, and Promoting Your Business* and the Podcast host for NAR's Center for REALTOR® Development. She has worked eighteen plus years as a successful real estate professional and ten years speaking nationally.

Monica's Story

My husband Mark has had chronic pain issues for a while. The event that magnified everything was a regular day waterskiing when suddenly he crashed into the water, detaching both his retinas. Because of an inaccurate doctor's diagnosis, by the time he had surgery on them, permanent damage had been done. The personal crisis was far greater for him. But this is about me. And, let's face it, family members' stories that relate to loved ones are seldom told.

My mother had been visually handicapped, so I was already in a mindset from childhood where I need to take care of everyone. In that sense, though, it was different and weird for me; it felt like another day of living with a problem that needs a solution. That is what I do— solve problems. But I couldn't solve his problems, and I am grateful to say he works on them daily.

For myself, I needed to first acknowledge that our situation had changed. It wasn't as bad as it could have been, but it was enough to take him out of the workforce and put us into a different lifestyle. I feel a bit bad sometimes because these challenges don't devastate me. I'm a naturally strong person and just keep moving on. What I would say though to anyone is that there is a grief process. At the minimum, we need to grieve what won't happen because of that change. Some things we had hoped for won't be like this now. And we need to let them go. We are going to move towards a new direction, and we may need to choose to recognize that there will be beauty and relationships on this new journey just as there would have been on the other journey.

I'm satisfied that we are both growing in it. I know that is hard for many people. Some people don't accept the changes and become bitter about their loss. We were already in a growth mindset that we had been developing, and gratefully, we had never lived in denial about hard things. Mentally we were somewhat prepared for change in whatever form it might take. But when there are surprises, you are never fully ready, so the grief and feelings can catch you off guard.

Life requires adjustment. That is a complete sentence. The line about "choose your hard" is very real. Pain is hard, anger is hard, working on your attitude is hard, eating well is hard. Everything is hard. So, choose your hard. Strive towards moving through the process, allowing yourself to feel and choosing to enjoy the good that is in your life. Or go and find the good.

I still grieve when I think of things that I wanted us to do together that we won't be able to do. I acknowledge it, express gratefulness for the good we have experienced, and look for a different way to satisfy the desire I have. Things we desire can be satisfied in more ways than people first think. Maybe we can still travel, but we need to do it differently than we had imagined before. Maybe we can't have people over to the house anymore, but we can have coffee out with friends.

How can I adapt and improve my situation? One of the adaptations we made, primarily for my husband, was to get a dog. He needed the company, and Charlie gives him purpose and a reason to take a walk every day. I didn't realize how much I would be blessed by the dog. We love to travel and getting the dog was a big stretch. Life changed though. He's been a good companion to us during this time.

My adjustments have been minimal because Mark has done so much work adapting to his situation. My contacts in a Facebook® chronic pain caregiver group have it so much tougher. Their partners don't do the work to create hope and improvement in their lives. So, they do all the work, give up all the dreams, and have a partner who just gripes and writhes in misery. That would be harder, and I'm not sure I would stay with that person after a reasonable period. Mark gives me space to do what I need to do. And over the years, he has sort of learned to tell me how he feels, so I get some insight—eventually.

I travel by myself more. He goes occasionally. I'm the sole breadwinner, but this is not a big deal for me, even though it may be for some people. He helps with the house, so that is a blessing for me. I feel grateful to still have a partner. We deal with what life shares with us together. For that I'm very grateful.

I think conversation about the inevitability of suffering might be appropriate. When people believe that life on earth can be "perfect" —whatever that is—they are surprised and saddened when suffering comes. And then they stay bitter because they are now denied a "perfect" life. Jesus and the Buddha both spoke much of the inevitability of suffering. The Book of Joy by the Dalai Lama and Archbishop Tutu has a whole chapter in it, which is very good. Much of the world finds joy in their "less fortunate" lifestyle because they expect it to be hard. They know life will be hard and they take joy in the daily beauty. Americans are a demanding and entitled culture and feel deprived when life is hard. Your starting point in a worldview matters.

Regret isn't really anything I think of anymore. As Mark says, "If you like who you are now, there should be no regrets." We calibrate our lives to a new normal.

What do we do if we don't want a new normal? We stay under the influence of the intense emotions we are experiencing like a mobius loop—a continuous never-ending tract, one emotion feeding upon another. Unless we take action to change our behavior and respond to a new way of life, we will continue to live in an unending cycle of grief that holds sadness, anger, and guilt preventing us to move to a place of letting go to finding a new way of coping with the loss.

After time has passed and the grief subsided, we can treasure the memories of losing a loved one by the lessons learned. Josh Cadillac, top selling real estate agent, entrepreneur, and author of RAD talks about how his dad impacted his life to become the person he is today.

Josh's Story

Some of the toughest things to learn in life have to be tenacity, perseverance, and determination. The only real way to learn these traits is to have to endure something hard. Many parents today try their best to insulate their kids from these types of experiences. My dad was not one of those parents as it turns out. My father was born in 1930 and therefore lived through the great depression, World War II, went to military school, and was drafted into the military during the Korean War. To say that he grew up and lived through tough times would be a bit of an understatement, and so this formed his ideas of what builds character in men. One of the first times I saw this was as a little boy of three or four. We were driving in the car, and we needed to get somewhere in a hurry because people were depending on us. I told my dad I needed to use the restroom. He looked at me and told me "Son, sometimes you need to learn to soldier." Those are words he used many times in my life when I had to deal with discomfort or something hard because the situation demanded it.

Throughout the course of my life, he would put me in situations that would push me and challenge me often to do more than I thought I could. As I got older the difficulty and the intensity of those situations only intensified because tenacity, perseverance, and determination are only honed by taking the next and bigger challenge. One time he had told me that we needed to take up the tile floor in the cafeteria we ran for a local school. The floor had a tile called VCT which is a thin asphalt/vinyl type of tile that adheres very well naturally. The only thing that makes it stick better than the adhesive they use to lay it is traffic and time. In other words, the longer it's down and the more people walk on it, the harder it is to get up. Did I mention this was in the cafeteria? The most highly trafficked room in the building, and it had been down for forty years.

We knew it would be tough to take up the 14,000 sq. ft. of tile, but we had the right tools, we thought. We had rented industrial tile scraper machines to get the floor up but unfortunately VCT was not what they had in mind when they made these machines. If you used the machine the way it was designed, it would just slide on top of the tile. In order to get it to remove the tile, we had to lift the scrapper off its wheels so that it just rested on the blade and then push it into the tile. This required holding the machines handle, which is vibrating like crazy, directly under our chin, for hours.

They had told us it would take a crew of guys a week to get the floors up, but we only had the weekend to get it done as the room had to be ready to use on Monday. I was at about fourteen or fifteen at this point. My dad had me rent two machines and me and a crew of three other guys started taking the floor up at 6:00 am on Saturday. The work took forever, was miserable, and the way we had to use the tools was super uncomfortable. No matter how much tile we took up, it never seemed like we were making progress.

There was an important life lesson I learned there though: If I kept looking at how far away the goal was, I never felt like I would get there, but when I looked back and saw all the tiles that had been removed, I knew progress was being made. Sometimes looking back can be a good thing to remind you of what you've overcome to get to where you are.

At midnight I sent my crew of guys home and told them I would finish the last few hours alone as they had families to go home to. At 4am my dad showed up with my little brother. They were there to "relieve" me. Now to be clear, I had been going for twenty-two hours straight at this point. I had about an hour to an hour and half's worth of work left. I looked at my dad and said, "get my brother out of here. I'm going to finish." He gave me a subtle nod of his head, acknowledging his respect for my decision, and left with my brother. Some people see cruelty in my father's actions, but I will tell you this: Surviving that floor showed me I was tough enough to survive many of the subsequent challenges life threw my way. My dad knew that is what I needed as a young man.

My dad wasn't the "all talk and no action" kind of guy though. He was never a tough guy for being a tough guy's sake either. He was a different kind of toughness. He never threatened to punch someone or start a fight. But if something needed to be done, it got done regardless of the cost. My dad was the kind of guy that did what he said he would do, and people could depend on him for that.

One time I clearly remember was near the end of Dad's life. The years had not been kind to his body. He had so much pain in his legs that the doctors thought he must have micro fractures in the bones. It was so bad and the pain medication they had was so insufficient for his agony that they were going to install a morphine pump inside his body to deliver morphine constantly so he could stand and walk. I was working in the family business, and we were shorthanded for a major outdoor catering event we needed to do. It was a huge job for the folks doing the setup and tear down as we needed to start at 6:00 am and the tear down was seldom completed before 2:00 am the following morning. A long day, to say the least.

I was in charge of the whole operation from start to finish. We had the people we needed to set up and tear down, but the service time was from 5:00 pm till 10:00 pm. We knew we didn't have enough people to get the food out as fast as we wanted to. We got the whole event set up and just before service time started, I saw my dad's Cadillac pull up. I saw this old man get out of the car, stand up straight, square his shoulders and do battle with himself one more time. He stood there from the start till the last person was served and never complained once— because sometimes you need to learn to soldier.

It has been a bit more than twenty years since my father passed away. I still miss him, his stories, his wisdom, and his quiet drive to always be a man to be counted on. It doesn't hurt the same way it did when we first lost him, but at times thinking of whether he would be proud of me is still enough to make me emotional. I love my dad, and I use his memory to drive me to be the type of guy he would have called "a good man." For his generation, there really wasn't higher praise one man could give another. So I go forward with the knowledge my dad is watching me from above, *and I try to give him a reason to smile, point, and say to anyone that will listen, "that's my boy."*

Reaching a place of acceptance in the grief process is reaching resolution and enacting a new normal that life goes on. A loved one becomes a part of your life, but in a different way.

Chapter 3

Signs of Being Emotionally Overwhelmed

In Chapter 2, we talked about the Stages of Processing Strong Emotions, and we read the life changing stories of how grief impacted people at various levels. After experiencing grief, there are new perspectives on life, but the journey is not easy to go through to get to a place of acceptance. Some people will make it through the grief process and others may get stuck. Reliving the past and constantly bringing up the person or event, as if the past is a part of the present, is likely being stuck in grief.

During a conversation with an older gentleman, he spoke about losing his son as if it were recent. When asked how long it has been, he said not too long ago, but after doing the calculation, we realized it was twenty-two years ago. His son died at the age of twenty-five, and the father could not let go of his son. Not being able to let go will cause a person to become stuck in grief which makes the grief complicated and difficult to resolve.

Reading an article from the Mayo Clinic, the author writes that "complicated grief, sometimes called persistent complex bereavement disorder...painful emotions are so long lasting and severe that you have trouble recovering from the loss and resuming your own life" (2022). To get to a place of acceptance of the person's death does not mean that you will let go and forget the person. On the contrary, it means that you have done the grief work and ready to move to another level of your life. As mentioned previously, grief comes in many forms: loss of loved ones, job termination or forced retirement, health issues, catastrophic events, economic loss, and so many other things.

The hardest thing we may have to do in our lives is to acknowledge our situation and subsequent emotions. Then we must do the work to evaluate our status quo to determine options and next steps. And yes, this is hard to do if you are crying all the time or isolating yourself from those who love you.

At some point, however, the crying does stop, and the internal panic recedes as we begin to stabilize.

How can we recognize we (or others) are in the throes of strong emotions when we are so close to the situation? We know our emotions can cloud reality. Our desire to reestablish stability in our emotions means we must be better at identifying the signs, which may be transitory or a constant underlying current that directs all decisions and personal perceptions. Consider the following as flares that are sent up and out to people we love, hoping they get the signal we are under a tsunami of emotions and need help.

Emotional

- Withdrawal from engaging with others in normal social situations.
- Crying or isolating yourself from enjoying happiness.
- Pouring over memories, photos, songs, videos of what was.
- Desperation which may manifest in frenzied efforts to fix situations.
- Fear or panic relating to loneliness or abandonment.
- Anger either aggressively towards self or others.
- Becoming "cause" focused, never letting this happen again to someone else.
- Acting like nothing happened (state of denial).
- Ongoing regret such as how we feel when we look in the mirror and see the 40 pounds we can't lose or the signs of aging.

Physical

- Weight loss—refusing to eat—nothing tastes right.
- Weight gain—food is a comfort. Something good in bad times.

- No attention paid to personal grooming—lack of showering, no makeup, or wearing the same outfit for several days.
- Picking fights with family members, friends, or strangers.

Mental/Spiritual

- Lack of interest in engaging with others and coveting isolation.
- Addiction
- Frenzied urge to uproot habits and dive head first into new experiences.
- Questioning personal beliefs on spirituality and relationships.

Our teachers, parents, and friends expose us to examples of how to experience strong emotions. We mimic what we see. If we are only exposed to anger or abandonment, are we doomed to repeat the cycle generationally?

We can't stop the negative ways of managing our emotions until we observe and understand how they manifest and the circumstances that allow sadness, regret, shame, rage, or depression to grow. The following is a list of ways our emotions manifest themselves to others and situations that amplify personal distress:

- **Abruptly Erupts with No Idea of Origin.** The pain of grief returns unexpectedly and harshly. For example, you are watching a movie and suddenly recall a conversation or experience that mirrors what is going on the big screen. The sorrow or regret surfaces quickly and we catch our breath bracing for the emotional assault. Walking down the street shopping and you turn to your loved one and say, "Mom will love that scarf!" and suddenly realize that your mother has died four years before. Talking as if she were still alive reopens a wound you thought you had buried. It leaves us with feelings of sadness, anger, confusion and missing what was.

- **Friendship Landmines**. We often feel we can treat our best friends any way we want, because we are friends, right? A true friend is like a loyal dog that no matter how many times they are abused, they come back for a pet on the head. Sometimes people in deep grief can't see they may be permanently damaging previously loving and supportive relationships.

- **Loss of Self-Identity / Purpose**. This can happen from experiencing a traumatic disability, unexpected job change, financial crisis, unrelenting criticism from mentors or co-workers, or transitioning into retirement. Often, we can feel sorrow or grief when we lose our internal compass. What used to make us jump out of bed every morning came from the fact that we were contributing to our family, community, or spiritual needs. We grieve when opportunity, options or best laid-out plans are rendered "cancelled." Working to validate ourselves in the eyes of others becomes problematic, especially if we can't figure out who we are anymore. When we look in the mirror we wonder "where did we go?"

- **Judging and Rejection.** Because we have endured the loss or experienced the life event that no one could possibly "get," we might decide that everyone comes up short. What others should have done, could have done and didn't do only increases the anger. We make the abrupt decision to remove them from our lives. It's simpler that way, right? Condemning others feels much better than being "attacked" or criticized ourselves.

- **Competition Escalates.** Desperation to take control back can penetrate every aspect of our lives. We start feeling a sense of jealousy and work diligently to "come out on top." That may appear as dominating conversations, dressing better, or having "nicer" things than other people. A mouse-like personality suddenly roars like a lion, making sure everyone notices them. They will not be overlooked or defeated.

- **Abusive Behavior / Mind Games.** We have all been on the receiving end of an unfiltered biting retort from a loved one. We shake our head and wonder "Where the heck did that come from?" Like throwing the television remote to the floor because emotions are so high, to some, violent action seems to be the only way to dissipate energy. We may "ghost" someone by dodging a call, make passive aggressive comments, act loving one moment and the next minute show the cold shoulder to people we care about. Playing mind games and disrupting relationships is a fear response. It's testing how far we can push someone to see who truly loves us.

- **Follow Wrong Advice.** In the aftermath of a traumatic event, we can become desperate for any guidance that will make us feel better or cure the situation. We may cling to questionable advice from "independent parties" and experience our loyal friend's frustration as they scream and shout against us taking that advice. We might think "What do they know? They haven't lived through what I have!" and we move forward into disaster anyway.

- **Emotionally Battered.** Being tired psychologically and physically shows itself in many forms: slowing speech patterns, withdrawal from social engagements, sleeping long hours or struggling to find that one peaceful place where no one will intrude on your thoughts. Consider the medical profession as it struggled to manage the COVID 19 crisis: life and death, every day, relentless and brutal. How can we not retreat from the world, hoping our personal cocoon will soothe away the anxiety and stress?

- **Unresolved Relationship Issues.** It's a well-known fact that the ones closest to us can wound us the most. Over the course of time, we experience a sibling or friend's behavior becoming aggressive or demeaning, especially when they interact with us. We know we must put boundaries in the relationship to "protect" our own emotions. What's left is an ongoing longing for a connection that we "wish" for, but we know won't improve. This results in an ongoing underlying river of regret that squeezes our heart every time we see that person. And if that person dies unexpectedly, the grief of never overcoming the barriers simmers below the surface, possibly for a lifetime.

- **Containing or "Burying" the Real You.** Trying to be something that others want us to be creates personal chaos. Conflicting emotions, sadness of not being able to express ourselves naturally and being accepted by others can lead to emotional strain which in turn manifests in physical distress. Perhaps your sense of humor is too frivolous for your serious, proper family or your flamboyant way of dressing just isn't right for the community you live in. Nothing like strangers giving you the side eye and taking joy in diminishing your personal choices by making you the center of their negative attention. Often the best humorous stories come from personal pain—ask any comedian who has learned to turn personal adversity into something magical.

Consider the obstacles you face when addressing your grief, stress, or realignment of your life purpose. It isn't a magic trick. It begins with knowing and accepting what you face and then determining how you move forward. What resources do you need and who can you count on to help you? Take accountability for your decisions and celebrate the wins. If something doesn't work, recalibrate, redirect, and reaffirm what you are trying to achieve. In the end, if we can't trust ourselves to make the right decisions for our well-being, then we must be brave enough to allow the right people to guide you.

Chapter 4

Addressing and Rebounding from Emotional Turmoil

Now comes the hard part—addressing when we are in the aftermath of grief that we need help and then doing something about it. Some of us are caught in an emotional trap that is due to a sudden unexpected occurrence and others will need to confront emotions buried for years. Either way, the struggle is real and will vary significantly from person to person. All we can hope for is some guidance on how to avoid the landmines in life or possible ways to come out in one piece.

CAMMIE'S STORY

One night I was the on-call chaplain when I received a phone call around 2:30 a.m., the nurse on duty said, "I need you to come to the unit right now. Patient X is crying uncontrollably, and I cannot get her to stop. She is asking for a chaplain." From experience in counseling patients, I knew that if I took time to race to the hospital and meet with her face to face, patient X would not want to talk. So, to take advantage of the moment and connect with her quickly, I asked the nurse to give the phone to the patient.

Patient X was hysterically crying as she described what happened. She had come into the hospital for surgery and during the night, she woke up suddenly because she remembered something that happened forty years ago. She recalled being at home with her family eating dinner when there was a knock at the door. Her husband went to the door and when he opened the door, shots fired and killed him right in front of his family. For forty years, she was estranged from her children and family so she could focus on getting revenge for her husband. Maybe being in a hospital was the trigger for her to recall memories from forty years prior.

The next morning, I went to see her, and she had shut down and would not talk with me. It was if the conversation that we had on the phone did not exist. Clinically, she made a slight breakthrough, but it would not last unless she was willing to talk. I offered to get a social worker or psychologist to come and talk with her, but she refused. To unpack forty years of trauma of seeing her husband killed in front of her would take time, and since she did not do anything for forty years, she may think it is not worth talking about. Fear may have kept her from facing the tragedy of losing her husband, and fear of the loss of her children that she abandoned when she became estranged from them.

Reaching out and then retreating is not unusual for people to do when confronting this type of profound experience. Grief gets hidden in different forms of emotions which can be mistaken for other reasons. If patient X wants to talk about the loss of her husband, she will do so when she is ready and hopefully, she will find someone who will listen and help her process her strong emotions in a positive and caring way.

IDENTIFY THE CORE PROBLEM

Unresolved emotions like grief are bad for your health and psychologically can prevent a person from achieving inner peace and contentment. Be brave, be objective and shine a light on your life. Is it fear, impatience, unrequited love (or friendship), or your consistency in acting as a victim rather than taking control over your decisions? Do a reality check of relationships, situations and plans interrupted to determine what you need to do. For patient X, we will never know how traumatic it was to see her husband killed in an instant. Forty years ago, patient X could have been seen as weak to get help, so she lived with the feelings of anger, guilt, sadness, isolation, depression, loneliness, estrangement, abandonment, and the list could go on.

ACKNOWLEDGE YOUR EMOTIONS

Grief may resurface by a trigger of a word or action, and it can startle you when it appears unexpectedly. Recognize grief when you experience it. How are you feeling: depressed, scared, lonely, or sad at your loss? Did a loved one pass and you failed to resolve issues before they died? Is regret driving your sadness? Were expectations of a job, weight loss program or family members something you feel stressed about?

Once we identify how our emotions impact us and how we extend that outward to those who love us, we can finally begin to find options and support. Don't blame yourself for having feelings. It means we have a capacity for empathy and connection to what others may also be experiencing in their lives.

Give yourself and others permission to grieve. Be patient during the grieving process with yourself and others. There is no set time for how long a person will grieve. When a person is in a prolonged state of grief, it's time for the person to seek help—with a good friend or a professional counselor. The person has to decide what is going to work best for them. Talking about grief with direction and guidance will help the person to see that there is life after a loss.

LET YOURSELF CRY

Society has trained us to not let others see us become emotional. We're not talking getting hysterical but just shedding tears because the emotions we are feeling are so strong, our body reacts naturally. Society discourages us to cry in the workplace as it's perceived as weakness by others. Sometimes others may want to blame you for crying, assuming you must have done something. Family, friends, and co-workers may tend to shy away from you because they think grief is contagious, and they, too, will start crying.

Haven't we witnessed a speaker whose voice catches in their throat when suddenly something about their topic reminds them of a person or situation? They don't sob, but it's very evident that what they are feeling is strong and real, that the grief is exhibited in their behavior. As they struggle to regain control and you are in that audience, doesn't your heart pause? Does your empathy for that person increase or do you feel slighted because they did not stay professional?

Simple fact—we are human.

Crying is the healing balm for the loss.

Emotions are part of our reality and are core to our personality. It's when crying becomes extreme and nonstop that we must seek help.

GET HELP—USE YOUR RESOURCES

Identify the help you need: read books, talk to friends or a trusted spiritual counselor, get professional counseling, or simply take a quiet moment for reflection by journaling, walking, or doing nothing. Set embarrassment or rationalization that you are tough enough to handle everything aside. If we don't acknowledge that we need help, we can possibly turn our individual situation into a crisis that magnifies not only our personal distress but may alienate others.

If you have a friend or family member who is in distress, be there for them. They don't need words really; all they may want is your quiet supportive presence. Let them be a mess for a while because it's part of healing.

Many of you have heard the story of Job in the bible. When Job was at his lowest point in life, his friends gathered to tell him that he must have done something wrong to be in the position of losing everything in life. His wife asked him, "Where is your God? Why don't you curse your God for what He has done?" Job would not allow himself to curse the Lord.

Despite pressure from his wife and friends, Job sat in his sorrow and grief. Then came a friend who would offer kind words by saying *nothing*. Sometimes, that is what we need from the visitor to say *nothing* and sit quietly with us. Saying nothing does not mean we don't care. It means I am present with you, and I am here for you. Job was feeling the loss of everything that he loved so dearly, and at the same time, he had to justify why he was feeling all the emotions of grief. Job responded by saying, "If you would only keep silent, that would be your wisdom!" (NRSV, Job 13:5).

Just getting through the day seems like eternity and then having to formulate your feelings into words when you don't know how you are feeling (overwhelmed, lonely, sad, unhappy, or angry) can be frustrating. Sometimes all you can do is try to put your thoughts in order as best as you can, but then we have to deal with others being uncomfortable and not knowing what to say.

Below is a short list of unfortunate words people might say during a loss or crisis.

- It will get better.
- The person is in a better place.
- You are strong and you will get through. this.
- Don't cry.
- It is time for you to step into the role of the person who died.
- Everyone dies.
- You knew this would happen.
- You will find somebody else.
- It was just a house.
- You need to get over this and move on with your life.
- It has been too long.

What if a person just comforted you by saying, "I am here for you. If you need someone to listen to your story, I will listen. If you need to sit quietly, I can do that. If you need to go for a walk, I will walk with you."

The Hallmark Staff says everyone deals with pain and hurt differently, and that there are universal languages that will help to sooth and comfort people during loss and crisis (2020).

For example:

- I am in this with you, I am here with you.
- I will listen if you need to talk.
- You are very important to me, and nothing will ever change that.
- Can I give you a hug?
- I want to be here for you, in whatever way is best for you.
- I'm going to be checking on you more, then commit to calling or making plans on a regular basis.

WHERE IS GOD IN TIMES OF SORROW AND PAIN?

We have heard "Life doesn't stop for anyone." How much time is sufficient for a person to grieve? In some religious traditions, people are given a year to grieve, and after the year anniversary, families will gather to have a service of remembrance. Religious beliefs differ from Eastern and Western faith traditions. Rituals are symbolic: covering mirrors in the home to hide the vanity, covering the front door indicating someone died in the family, stopping the clocks in the home. The rituals can help in the grieving process because people are gathering to either celebrate or remember the life of the person. Religious beliefs can come in conflict with the grieving process if people don't believe in the rituals. Just like a person would seek mental health professional, it is similarly important for a person to talk with a religious leader who can best help to understand the faith tradition if questions are involved.

A frequent phrase used in times of loss and crisis is "Where is God?" If this question does not get resolved, the grief process could become delayed. People will move more towards faith and others will move away from faith.

What is common during the grieving process is anger, and being angry with God is part of the emotional turmoil of grief. Yet, you will hear people say, "You cannot be angry with God."

It took over twenty years for R.F. Smith, Jr., a Baptist pastor, to write about losing his son. Smith wrote *Sit Down, God…I'm Angry,* and in his book he talked about how the loss of his eighteen-year-old son had a tremendous effect on him upholding his belief in God. Smith grew up in the 1950's where it was blasphemy to speak ill of God. Yet, this pastor used his anger to get closer to God by putting God on the witness stand to answer why the Lord would allow his child to be taken from the family. It was forbidden territory for a pastor and a Baptist pastor to bring God to the witness stand. People are so afraid to ask God "Why?" but when they listen, God has the answers.

CAMMIE'S STORY

In 1996, I was too young to be confronted with the death of losing my mother. I expected my mother to be with me for many years to come. I was working on an MBA. It was in the spring of

1996 when my mother was taken to the emergency room and within two days, she would undergo triple bypass surgery. Two weeks after being released from the hospital, she went for a check-up. After returning home, my sister noticed that she was carrying a fever, so we took her back to the hospital, and she was admitted for the night.

Every time I hear the opening song on the Golden Girls, I receive flashbacks to the night when we received a call from my sister, Pauline, who was at the hospital with my mom. My sister said, "The nurse found an infection in the incision and the doctor has ordered Mommy to undergo emergency surgery right away." We all rushed to the hospital with my dad who had become frail and weak. He could barely stand up; yet he was not going to stay home while his wife of almost sixty years was fighting for her life.

My mom transferred from the local hospital to a larger hospital where the surgery was scheduled at 1:00 a.m. that morning. As my mom was being prepped for surgery, I remembered her family doctor came to be with us. It was comforting knowing that he was there with us. He offered to lead us in prayer. When the doctor said, "Not my will but thy will be done," I could hear myself screaming on the inside NO. Not God's will. God had done enough by making her go through triple bypass surgery and now emergency surgery that we could lose her. I recall thinking, "No God, how am I to believe that I can trust You?"

I did not know it at the time, but I was in so much pain and screaming out to the Lord, I was being brought closer to God rather than farther away. My mom had to go through two additional surgeries within three days. The infection around her heart was life threatening, and the doctors had to reenter to clean out the infection. The family kept vigil in the waiting room day and night. Some of us could not bear seeing her with her heart exposed with bandages covering the incision. After the third surgery, she was in a coma. It took weeks before she gained consciousness. Then she was moved to a rehab hospital to learn how to walk and use motor skills.

She came home around her birthday, June 20. I asked my dad if we could have a birthday party for her and he said yes. We invited the ICU nurse to the party. While the nurse was there, she noticed that my mom's skin color and eyes were jaundiced. The following day, I took my mom to the hospital where she was admitted for the doctors to run tests. The test results came back that she had terminal cancer, with four to eight weeks to live.

Where is God? Where are you God? In my grief, I became so angry that God would put her through so much. I wanted to know, for what reason? I went on a quest to find God. It was not an easy journey. I could not continue with my studies in business, so I dropped all my classes that spring. What I have learned is don't go looking for God because you might find yourself getting closer to the Lord. In August of 1996, I enrolled in another master's program. I went to Divinity School. I called Howard University School of Divinity my sanctuary, a place where I was walking on sacred grounds. The location was a monastery prior to *the school. I found a place where I could be accepted in my pain and quest for understanding about human pain and suffering. I could ask questions of my professors, and I did.*

Right after her death in September of 1996, I could not shed a tear. I became stoic with emotions because that is how I managed life issues in the past and that is how I knew to cope. I knew I should cry, but I could not cry. For almost three months, I walked through life like it was just another ordinary day. Then in December of the same year, something made me afraid and triggered feelings of fear. I fell apart. I was taken to the hospital and life has not been the same. I started to cry which opened a flood gate of tears for me to start grieving. It has been twenty-seven years since my mom passed, and I can say that working through the pain and hurt by embracing and remembering my mother's love and care has made me who I am today.

GET UP AND MOVE ON

You've let your emotions out. Now what? Wipe off the tears, straighten your shoulders and start planning your move forward. Seek hope from any resource that resonates with you. Is it religion and seeking your path to God, or can you find it in the smile of small child? Taking care of others may be the salve you need so perhaps dedicating yourself to a life of service will give you purpose and meaning. It may be as simple as finding an emotional support animal who adores you without any ties attached. There are contradictions we face every day in our lives and many roads lead spiritually to God. Believing there is only one way, one path to hope, makes it substantially harder to overcome sadness and may in turn embed another level of grief in unfulfilled expectations.

We don't assume that this process will be an easy one. But if you don't take the first steps to at least try to overcome your overwhelming emotions and recalibrate your expectations, it is possible to dig a deeper well of despair. Being a victim is the easy way. Living an enlightened, emotionally secure life takes work and dedication to the healing process.

Chapter 5

Embracing Inconvenience— Living a Quality Life

When emotions run rampant, we can either succumb to the onslaught of overwhelming feelings or we can stand up and declare "enough already!" Laying trampled, weak, and broken might be the easier way to manage crisis, but, remaining a victim usually only compounds issues, not resolves them. Focusing on how we can attain and maintain a quality life can provide us with options and opportunities that may have not existed previously. Addressing the impact of the negative experiences is not only character building, but it can also strengthen our resolve to design worthy outcomes and expectations. In effect, we can recalibrate our lives to a new normal and achieving individual contentment regardless of outside influences.

Consider the following:

VALIDATING YOUR EMOTIONS

There is a reason why you are feeling what you are feeling. Own it. Take an unfettered look at your childhood and current life.

- Was your upbringing chaotic?
- Were you abandoned by someone you loved and continue to seek a way to fill that hole?
- What support system did you have growing up and what do you have now?
- Did you use passionate outbursts to achieve a goal or get something you wanted? How is that working for you now?
- Did you react emotionally because that is what others expected of you?
- Was your home life a haven? If not, how did you handle the uncertainty of not feeling safe?
- Did you and do you have advocates? How does that make you feel, and do you honor loyalty in your life?

Whatever the answers may be, understanding your perceptions and corresponding emotions creates the building blocks on how you react to traumatic or tumultuous situations.

RECOGNIZE YOUR RESILIENCY ABILITY

The first step is honestly evaluating your ability to manage crisis. What type resonates with you?

- **Retreat**. You have lived your life defensively; experiencing so many episodes of trauma you become resigned to being life's punching board and quickly retreat emotionally to protect yourself.

- **Freeze**. You have been fortunate to have led a charmed life, and when a stressful, unexpected situation arises, may feel totally unprepared to manage the emotional toll the crisis demands. Therefore, you act as if nothing has happened. If we can just skip over the bad parts by not acknowledging our emotions, we can move forward.
- **Resist.** You are a natural born fighter. Trauma is something to be conquered. You are the caretaker, not the one who needs to be taken care of. You may feel that having emotional outbursts don't solve the problem. Instead, maintaining a clear headed, rational approach to handling grief or depression begins with a plan of attack.

Let's be direct. We have the right to give ourselves permission to feel. Experience the sadness, depression, worry, or stress that a situation squeezes from us. As you know, trauma is defined and experienced differently for each person and the level of emotional energy they put into the situation will vary significantly. The question is *how* you bounce back and regain control of your feelings.

ACCOUNTABLE FOR DECISIONS AND RELEASING GUILT

The big question, it seems, is are you truly helpless in the face of crisis? Why do some lean into a situation and others walk away? Have you accepted responsibility for your part in a conflict or acknowledge the outcome of decisions made?

For example, a person may feel guilty for not addressing and resolving familial conflicts before a loved one dies. Is it the pain of regret for not having done something that takes people off the deep end? The burden of guilt can be crippling. Looking rationally at your relationships, you may find that often you weren't the one in control. Decisions made by other people created a negative dynamic. And, in retrospect, we grow to understand we can't save everyone, no matter how much we try.

Nola is a successful, professional businesswoman and a self-proclaimed "doer." As a tremendous student of life, she is diligently learning the art of "being." A lifelong Oregonian, Nola is a daughter, a sister, and a mother.

Nola's Story

My situation has been ongoing since about 2017, though it is only in hindsight that timeframe becomes clear. In 2019, my mom's behaviors, which had always been challenging, became monumentally worse, and frankly bizarre. At the time, I really believed it was me. My mother didn't like me, and she couldn't tolerate me or function around me. Weird for a mother to be that way, but I had learned to live with it. Sort of.

In September 2019, I'd flown to Ft. Smith, Arizona to attend to my special needs sister, something I'd done in conjunction with my mom's and her husband's requests and financial assistance for several years. I'd stayed with my folks prior to my flight out and planned to upon my return as well. The situation was so awful that I opted to go to the airport some twelve hours early and wait for my flight versus staying in my parents' home. Upon my return, I immediately drove to my own home—across the state—in the middle of the night. At that point, I decided to minimize any phone calls or visits with Mom.

Prior to Christmas 2019, my family and I stopped over to see my folks before flying to New Orleans on a Christmas Getaway. We visited only long enough to take them to dinner then we headed to an airport area hotel for our very early flight the next morning. Mom was agitated and accusatory during the short visit and at one point, while we four and her husband were visiting at their kitchen table, mom covered her ears and started yelling, "I cannot stand all this noise, why don't you just stop?" We said our goodbyes and wished them a Merry Christmas.

In February 2020, I received a phone call from a financial institution and from my mom which I could not understand. The bank representative wanted to "sell" them a product that made no sense for them and would have tied up their liquid assets at a time when they were both retired and did not have other means. The bank rep reported, "She did not seem to comprehend what was being said and she seemed to contradict herself a number of times." Shortly after, mom called and was verbally abusive and accusatory, "I didn't know you'd tied up all our money! We cannot do anything we want to with our own money!"

Within days, I went to Portland and had intended to take them to the bank to find out what the situation was. She refused *to go. I took her husband, discovered what was occurring, and he agreed not to change anything. He didn't understand what the rep was trying to accomplish. I did ask the rep to take them off their lists for "recommendations."*

In March 2020, her husband called me and said, "I just don't know what to do with your mom." Her verbal abuse and spending had markedly increased. Her husband was eighty-nine years old. The pandemic was just being talked about, though information was unclear. Oregon was to lockdown beginning March 28, and I decided to go and stay with my parents through the lockdown, which I understood would be just a couple of weeks.

Mom was not happy I was heading to Portland, but I needed to understand the situation, and to help her husband, as it was becoming clear that this behavior wasn't directed only at me.

Upon arrival, I found her husband in a state of failure to thrive. Mom was either sleeping or yelling all the time with not much in between. I contacted her primary care provider – a nurse practitioner who was at the end of her career, and, in my opinion, was fatigued by mom's behaviors. Mom, then 76, was out of control. I worked with the PCP to have them both evaluated neurologically and in every other way. I was able to get my mom's husband back to a baseline through daily walks and not allowing him to take medications that mom believed he needed (her information source largely being TV commercials). He shared his experiences with her, and I simply listened and did my best to hide my disbelief. The behaviors he shared were bizarre. And, not just recently, but for years and years.

She continued to spiral. She had been treated for depression for some years—I don't know how long—and had been seeing a therapist, but she proudly bragged to neighbors and others how she manipulated the therapist into to telling her own stories and thus didn't have to share hers. Neighbors reported her angst and started avoiding her. She was not allowed to play mahjong at the community center any longer—and this had nothing to do with the pandemic.

At the start of May, while still in lockdown, a close friend of mine who is a geriatric social worker, encouraged me to get mom see a neuropsychologist. I was able to get the referral from her PCP and to take her in for testing. The appointment was literally one day before I was to return to my own home. I took mom, waited two hours in the waiting room, and after the appointment, on the drive to her home, Mom described the testing and questions that he'd asked including whether she had visual and/or auditory hallucinations – both of which she told me she had answered yes. This was the first time she'd ever stated such.

I returned home the following day, not knowing what any of this had meant. Of note, since 2014, I was the durable power of attorney for both parents, medical and financial. This followed multiple hospital stays in which mom was on ventilators for various length of times.

In the middle of June 2020, mom was diagnosed with Lewy Body Dementia, which I'd never heard of. The PCP called her in, gave her the diagnosis, put her on rivastigmine, told her not to drive, and sent her on her way. Yep, she drove herself home. Mom did not tell her husband, nor me. The PCP did not call me nor even provide a message to me through MyChart. I discovered the diagnosis in MyChart and messaged the PCP to discuss and to find out what the next steps were. To which I received a response of, "your mother has seen every specialist available, what more do you want?" I asked for the neurophysiologist's report and received it.

This began a two-year journey of discovering what Lewy Body Dementia is and how to manage the symptoms, as there is no cure.

During most of the seven weeks living in their home, I was unable to care for my own confusion, grief, and upset. And frankly that has only shifted slightly over the last ten months (since April 2022), in that I got them placed into an assisted living community on my side of the state. I also began intensive therapy.

After I was able to return home, I mentally churned over my own immediate family members, work, and my relationship with Mom. I struggled between feeling bad for her, worrying that I'll "get it," and deflecting the verbal blows that she continued to volley my way. I didn't recognize that I was grieving and certainly could not have named the source of that grief at that time.

I've always been a doer, so I did, and then I did more, and when that didn't work, I did even more. I'd been attempting to change careers to do something I have a passion for. I even retained the services of a great mentor who is successful in the career I wished to move into. My own business (I'm self-employed with my husband) was booming, and my youngest was getting ready to finish college and move to Tucson to live with her sister. This would be a great time to change careers and really shine. I finally discovered that no matter how fast I am, I cannot outrun the underlying grief, caused from long-standing abuse, and amplified by her LBD diagnosis.

We launched our youngest daughter, who is thriving and returning for her master's in Tucson. I "stood-up" to my mom and took control getting them into assisted living with the help of some amazing doctors and caregiving study programs. I switched "umbrella" organizations to re-focus on launching my next career. Since the start of 2023, I have discovered the underlying grief. I am learning how to let go of the fantasy about my mom, and to tell the truth about how I was raised. I am the caregiver of an abuser.

To recalibrate, I've realized that no matter how I wish and hope for something different, she is who she is, and my acknowledging that doesn't mean that I must stop caring for her. Her reality is she has no one else, and her husband now has dementia as well. He too has no family who is willing to step up and step in. I've decided to continue to care for them both—with boundaries.

And while I will not shout it from the rooftops, I know that I must not hide this, the abuse, the behaviors, my own grief. When I keep this hidden, I find all kinds of reasons for her to be "right" and me to be "wrong." And the cycle continues.

My biggest regret is about time. I regret not being able or willing to face reality much sooner in my life. My counselor encourages me to have compassion for myself, and that I understood.

I regret not seeing my own inherent worth, simply for being human. I regret the overdoing I've done.

I have made so many significant changes. But those were really gates opening to allow me to "be" a bit more. I walked the Camino with my eldest daughter in June 2022. I generally stop working by 5 p.m. each day, and I take time for exercising and enjoyment activities. I practice Buddhism. I joined several support groups specifically for caregivers of those with dementia. I read and listened to those stories. I took up sewing and my Doggerchiefs By Nola are in high demand locally.

Regarding mom, I still care for her and her husband. I take them to all their doctor's appointments and shop for them. I pay their bills and manage everything that the assisted living facility cannot.

I no longer expect a relationship, and I understand and accept the "relationship" is transactional. They have needs, I fulfill them. However, I do so secondary to my own needs. Because they are safe, sometimes I choose not to pick up the phone when she calls. When I do pick up the phone or return the call, I ensure that I am in a good, protected space. I try to remember that she no longer has a choice about what she says (or does), the Lewy Body Dementia has taken that choice from her (if she ever had a choice).

I feel the grief, which comes in waves, and I remember that I am good and worthy, just by being human. I tell the truth, with those to which it would matter. This cannot be shared with just anyone. I believe we all share some common traits of grief, but what is very individualistic is the timing. Some folks just aren't ready to hear another's grief and those folks aren't often ready to feel their own. I've discovered, however, that there are a lot more people who are not only ready, but they need to hear others' grief stories to acknowledge their own.

WHO IS PAYING FOR YOUR GRIEF?

Swamped with emotion, it's very difficult to acknowledge how our behavior may be impacting others. If we are tangled up with grief, trapped in angry outbursts, or embroiled in behavior which subsequently demeans others, those closest to us may abandon you. It takes the stalwart heart to handle abuse, long term sorrow, and a negative relationship. People want to feel happy, to feel settled, appreciated, and loved. If we're embroiled in deep emotional outbursts for long periods of time, our health can also be negatively impacted.

Who in your life is paying for your emotional turmoil, children, spouse, friends, or co-workers? Once you identify your impact on others, you can hold a mirror up and recognize your role and impact on their lives. It's a hard step to take, but once it's done, you can work to repair the damage that has been done by simply thanking them for sticking with you.

THE POWER OF JOURNALING

Many people have found perspective, solace, and direction by writing down their feelings daily. Bring into the daylight how your emotions fluctuate.

- Define the purpose and intent of how you want to feel emotionally as you work through your healing process.
- Identify the cause of your feelings. Is it something you can control or not?
- Determine your role in why those emotions may be surfacing.
- Create actions and activities that will help you to stable ground.

By allowing yourself to be fully present in the moment and letting life happen, you'll begin to understand and accept the ebb and flow of your life. It's different for everyone. Spending energy to envy what someone else has is a waste of time.

Your life is yours. Your decisions, actions and ultimate intent can provide the roadmap to your new reality. By leaving room for the unexpected, both good and bad, we absorb lessons from all situations.

According to Harvard Medical School, "Some research suggests that disclosing deep emotions through writing can boost immune function as well as mood and well-being. Conversely, the stress of holding in strong feelings can ratchet up blood pressure and heart rate and increase muscle tension" (2016). The article recommends journaling as a way of releasing emotions. Below are three methods suggested:

1. Although writing about grief and loss can trigger strong emotions—you may cry or feel deeply upset—many people find journal writing valuable and meaningful, and report feeling better afterward.

2. Truly let go. Write down how you feel and why you feel that way. You're writing for yourself, not others. Don't worry about the grammar of sentence structure.

3. Try writing for fifteen to thirty minutes a day for three to four days, or as long as a week if you feel writing continues to be helpful. You could also try writing for fifteen to thirty minutes once a week for a month. One review of research on journal writing found that writing has stronger effects when it extends over more days. Source: Harvard Medical School

Cammie shared how journaling helped her when she wrote about her deep feelings of grief. There were times when she could not write a full sentence so she wrote what she could even if it was just a word—lonely, sad, isolated, depressed. She found solace in being able to address her feelings in a safe space. Through her journaling, she was able to express her thoughts safely.

Chapter 6
Quest for Healing

The goal, we can agree, is to enjoy our lives, in whatever fashion or shape that may take. That may not be as easy as we might think. Some of us are retired and discovering more alone time than we had counted on. Our children and friends are so busy living their own lives, we sometimes feel a bit neglected and lonely. Finding ways to fill up a day can be challenging, especially if we don't want to break the now "fixed income" bank. Mourning for lost connections can seep in, embedding itself into all aspects of living.

Our quest for healing begins with us being more receptive to what is going on around us and being open to opportunity. It includes a willingness to start doing something now rather than waiting for a more opportune time. How do we know if we like something unless we try it?

It starts with us acknowledging the search for healing may result in us losing something in order to gain something in return. For example, by cutting toxic people out of your life, you open the emotional space for genuine, supportive relationships. Consider how much better you would feel if you lost eighty pounds (or however many you need to lose) and see a healthy face and body reflected in the mirror? Throwing away all the clothing items that are XXL feels like shedding your old self. Sure, the weight loss process isn't easy or fun, but the feeling of accomplishment amplifies our sense of self-worth and esteem.

Enduring a trauma like Missy when she lost her house didn't mean the end for her. It began a shift in her life that very well may mean exciting, vibrant things for her. She is now in the mindset of moving forward instead of wallowing in the past.

If we can't release those strong emotions and find a path forward, we lose the person we are and who we are intended to be. Our identity and place in the world become compromised when we hit the pause button for too long.

POWER OF CONNECTION —THE HUMANITY FACTOR

As we wrap up this conversation, we can't avoid talking about how important it is to stay connected with others. Some have a very personal relationship with God, while others have a universal viewpoint that is outside religious institutions. Either way, many people believe that something more is out there. What that looks like is different for all of us. But we must acknowledge one simple fact:

Humanity thrives when *we* take care of each other.

It's our belief that there is a spark of God in each person. Whether that's described as an energy we emit, an emotional pull or commonality of an experience, we understand innately what people go through. Our empathy expands beyond our community when we cringe horrified at the devastation of a natural disaster. It's difficult to review the history of our country and the wrongs inflicted on people who happen to be different or less fortunate. That's because we wonder, "what if that was us?"

Our spark of connection thrives if we are emotionally open to others. Will we be hurt sometimes? Yes. But is it possible that your empathy at just the right moment may be a life-changing event for someone else? And is it possible that this person you connected with, in turn, helps someone else? The ripple effect of actions, intent and decisions is far reaching and a powerful aspect of humanity.

What impacts one, impacts all. Some call it the God spark.

- Live your life with wonder.
- Create your inner fortress of positive strength and become someone others can rely upon.
- Cry when you feel like it.
- Be depressed if you need to be.
- Seek help without shame.

- When your emotions run rampant, accept that a new normal is in play. Life can get easier through perspective. We can acknowledge that our loved one is no longer with us or that we got fired from a job we love, or our medical condition is deteriorating. Each reality check provides room to develop resolve.
- Know that our loved ones are never truly gone because we keep them close to our hearts. We remember them and smile.
- Realize that we may have lost a job, but we are capable and can get another that we will love just as much! Or, just maybe, we do something else that fully utilizes all our. skills.
- Realize that our medical condition is what it is, so what equipment and medical support is needed to thrive? Or what decisions need to be made to prepare for death?
- An environmental event destroys everything you have and the overwhelming support from the community and outsiders will bolster your belief in human kindness. People give when they can. Accept graciously because that is the God spark at work.

Ultimately, it's up to you to decode your life. What wonderous things await you if you make room for things to happen and accept those changes and challenges with open arms. You just might find out something profound.

You are worthy.

Chapter 7

Transitioning and Releasing the Real You

It's time to release the real you. Look into what was and start to define what will be. Answer these questions that will allow you to explore more deeply into what you value and what your intentions are for all levels of your life. Take a moment now to delve into and define the specifics that make up your reality and re-define your sense of purpose.

Remember—you are the only one who can take back control of your own life.

1. What are you passionate about? It ranks high on your priority scale.

2. What makes you proud?

3. What do you want to achieve? Why is that important to you?

4. What talents are you proud of? Is this something others know about you? If not, why not?

5. What personal characteristics do you want to change and why?

6. What type of people do you associate with?

7. Who are your greatest supporters?

8. Who are the people you trust? List them specifically. Why do you trust them?

9. Who in your life stops your personal development? Why do you let them?

10. Who is a coach or mentor whose ethics you value? Why do they stand out?

11. How do others describe, define, or perceive you? Is this what you intend?

12. What is your greatest fear and why?

13. How are your fears guiding your life? Is it something you can control?

14. List your greatest successes and how do you feel about them?

15. What are your strengths that others perceive you to have?

16. List your values (i.e., integrity, honesty, etc.)

17. Identify those trains and passions you will incorporate as part of your everyday life.

18. Define your personal code of ethics (how you would behave if your actions would never be discovered).

19. Describe a situation that created a personal ethical dilemma and how you handled it. Were you satisfied with how it was resolved? If you faced this dilemma today, would your approach be different and how?

20. If you change nothing in your life's direction, what's the worst-case scenario? Can you live with it? By staying in the same situation and doing nothing, will it cause a decline in your personal health or create undesired turmoil in your family?

21. What dreams do you regret not pursuing or what aspirations have you neatly tucked away and forgotten about, due to various roadblocks in life? What derailed your plans?

22. When did you first hear "You can't do that anymore?" How did that make you feel?

23. Do you like yourself as an adult? Or do you want to regain/recover the qualities you had as child? What were they?

24. Have you balanced your perceptions and desires with reality?

25. Do you live a life that reflects your values and do your circle of friends share those values?

26. Do you want others to know the real you? If not, what are you truly afraid of?

27. How and why have you modified your looks, ideas, or personality? How did this provide security and confidence for you?

28. How can you change your life so that you are playing your game and not someone else's?

29. How will others be impacted by your decision to change? What emotions surface and why do you feel that way?

30. What do you consider a devastating type of rejection and why would it be devastating to your esteem?

31. What actions/decisions have you taken/made in your life where you knew there would be an adverse outcome, but you did it anyway?

32. What actions or decisions have you made where there was some adverse outcome that you did not anticipate? After such an adverse outcome, did it become "obvious" that such an outcome could have been predictable?

33. Do you allow others to make you unhappy? Describe your situation specifically. What would happen if you spoke up/altered the dynamics?

34. List three positive actions you will commit to in achieving your personal healing.

35. Identify two ways to engage the support of your family and friends in reaching your goals.

36. What steps can you take to establish your legacy? How do you wish to be remembered and are you living that life?

37. What are three things you will commit to in the next year to accomplish – your personal bucket list.

38. What are your life goals?

39. What were the last five choices you made that gave you a sense of autonomy in your life?

40. To you, a peak period of happiness is when

As we conclude this book, think if there is any unfinished business in your life that you didn't get to complete because of a disruption. What are you going to do?

CAMMIE'S STORY

While authoring this book, I realized that my unfinished business was finishing the MBA that I withdrew from when my mom was dying. I answered God's call and pursued a different path of study, but I did not complete the MBA. In 2022 on my birthday, January 10, I started an MBA and finished on March 4, 2023. Accomplishing this degree was different, and it is because I finished what was unfinished in my life.

ABOUT THE AUTHORS

Karel Murray

An accomplished author and humorist, Karel presented nationally and internationally.

She is the author of:

- *When Emotions Run Rampant*
- *The Language of Intent: How Self Talk Transforms Outcome*
- *Conquering the Witch Within: Intergenerational Workplace Strategies that Get Results*
- *Hitting Our Stride: Women, Work, and What Matters*
- *Straight Talk: Getting Off the Curb*

Karel is a featured author in:

- *Extreme Excellence: Dynamic Interviews with America's Top 10 Performance Experts*

- *Ovation: How to Present Like a Pro by Len Elder*
- *Crystalline Moments: Discover Your Opportunities and Create Your Best Self by Coni Meyers.*
- *My Glasses Are on Top of Your Head: Tales of Life, Longevity and Laughter by Brenda Elsagher*

Karel holds a BA in human resources and has earned numerous designations and certifications in the speaking industry, served as Past President of the Real Estate Educators Association and Chairperson of the Blue Springs Chamber of Commerce. Karel is a DREI Emeritus (Distinguished Real Estate Instructor).

Her résumé includes experience as a human resources regional executive of a large commercial insurance firm, as an award-winning salesperson, as a manager of a top-producing real estate office, and as past owner of Our Branch, Inc., a national and international speaking, and training company.

Cammie Reed

Cammie has lived in the Washington, D.C. area since age ten when her parents moved from Georgetown, Guyana, South America. As a child, she loved the Seawall as she watched the waves, and as an adult, she embraces the peace and tranquility of how water brings a connection to hope and renewal.

Cammie's journey has taken her through many career paths as a pastor, clinician, educator, broker/owner, national speaker, and author, all which have defined a meaningful purpose in her life.

She is a broker/owner for a real estate brokerage and school. She is licensed in many states from Pennsylvania to

Florida and holds countless NAR designations. Cammie is a Distinguished Real Estate Educator (DREI).

She is the president and founder of Nani House whose mission is to help individuals and families with basic needs, food, clothing, and housing.

She is trained in NLP (Neuro-Linguistic Programming), Group Psychotherapy, Zen Therapy, Negotiation, and Mediation/Conflict Resolution. She is a well-recognized speaker at the local, state, and national levels.

She has degrees in business (BS & MBA), counseling (MS) and theology (MDiv & DMin) from the University of Maryland, Columbia College, Loyola University and Howard University, respectively.

Cammie's goal is to visit all fifty states to learn about various cultures and lifestyles. She lives in Maryland with her husband and youngest son, with her oldest son living close by. Family is an integral part of her life.

References

American Psychological Association. (2023). *Grief.* Retrieved from https://dictionary.apa.org/grief

Bialik, M. (2020). *A Brief History of Grief.* Retrieved from https://www.bialikbreakdown.com/articles/a-brief-history-of-grief.

Browne, D. (2020, July 31). *Hoarding Understanding and Treating.* Healthline. Retrieved from https://www.healthline.com/health/hoarding

Hallmark Staff. (2020, December 18). *Comforting Words: What to Say and Do in Tough Times.* Retrieved from https://ideas.hallmark.com/articles/encouragement-ideas/comforting-

Harvard Medical School. (2016, November 15). *Writing to Ease Grief and Loss.* Harvard Health Publishing. Retrieved from https://www.health.harvard.edu/mind-and-mood/writing-to-ease-grief

Keller, S. (2022, May 12). *Guilt versus Shame.* The Center for Loss and Bereavement. Retrieved from https://bereavementcenter.org/blog.

Kubler-Ross, E. (1996). *On Death and Dying.* Scribner Publishing: New York.

Mayo Clinic. (2016, October 19). *What is Grief?* Retrieved from www.MayoClinic.org

Mayo Clinic. (2022, December 13). *Complicated Grief.* Retrieved from https://www.mayoclinic.org/diseases-conditions/complicated-grief/symptoms-causes/syc-20360374

Meeks, W. (1993). *New Revised Standard Version (NRSV)*. The HarperCollins Study Bible, New York: HarperCollins Publishers.

Rosenfeld, L. (2018, November 29). *The Fire That Changed the Way We Think About Grief.* The Harvard Crimson. Retrieved from https://www.thecrimson.com/article/2018/11/29/erich-lindemann-cocoanut-grove-fire-grief/

Smith, R.F. Jr. (1997). *Sit Down, God…I'm Angry.* Judson Press: Valley Forge, PA.

Westberg, G. (1962). *Good Grief.* Fortress Press: Philadelphia.

If you have found this book to be helpful—

If you like what you read, and you want to order books for your friends, visit

HugoHouseBookstore.com
BarnesandNobles.com
Amazon.com

If you would like to order this book in bulk, please contact the publisher:

Patricia@HugoHousePublishers.com.

www.ingramcontent.com/pod-product-compliance
Lightning Source LLC
LaVergne TN
LVHW041337080426
835512LV00006B/506